Youth in Action

The Duke of Edinburgh's Award Scheme 1956–1966

DAVID WAINWRIGHT

Youth in Action

The Duke of Edinburgh's Award Scheme 1956–1966

WITH AN INTRODUCTION BY SIR JOHN HUNT

 HUTCHINSON OF LONDON

HUTCHINSON & CO (*Publishers*) LTD · 178-202 Great Portland Street London W1
London · Melbourne · Sydney · Auckland · Bombay · Toronto · Johannesburg · New York

First published 1966

c

This book has been set in Times, printed in Great Britain on Antique Wove paper by Anchor Press, and bound by Wm. Brendon, both of Tiptree, Essex

Acknowledgements

The author gratefully acknowledges permission from
Jonathan Cape Limited and Mr Arnold Wesker to
quote a speech from his play *Roots*.

PHOTOGRAPHIC CREDITS

Illustrations between pp. 16 and 17 are by Frank
Buck. Those between pp. 48 and 49, and 80 and 81
taken at the Park Gate Iron and Steel Company
Limited, Rotherham, are by the Gamma Group of
Guildford. The end-papers are by Thomas A. Wilkie
of Guildford. Other photographs are by agencies or
newspapers as indicated.

Contents

Introduction
by Sir John Hunt

I like the title of this book.

We live in a society whose compelling motive to action is competition. Success is rightly attributed to those who come high in examination results, who excel in standards of technical and sporting skill, who sell the most consumer goods and who submit the lowest tenders. There is, of course, nothing new about this; it is not to decry competition to observe that it has its origin in the law of the jungle. Few would deny its effectiveness in terms of stimulating standards of excellence; or claim that competition is wrong when conducted under strict rules, based on a universally accepted moral code.

But the fact is that we do not yet have such a code. And in a free society one danger is that too much value and esteem tend to be attached to those groups and individuals who attain success through competition; too little importance is given to those who are thus deemed to fail. So much may be at stake that rules and codes become obstacles in the rat-race, to be circumvented at all costs. In an age of ever-developing technology, those who cannot aspire to higher education are in danger of being considered less important to society. In a major group enterprise, those less highly skilled tend to be considered less as individuals in their own right, more as cogs in the machine.

Against this latter tendency our society has evolved, and is continually evolving, material safeguards. But today we still have to produce more adequate safeguards, of quite another order, for the many individuals who, because of the sheer scale of industrial enterprise, are unwittingly made to feel they do not matter. We have to re-establish the value of those who, for reasons of temperament, talent or scruple, do not succeed through competition, in earning a place in the sun of human esteem. This often-misplaced sense of failure—of not mattering—with its outcome in frustration, boredom and despair and the many specious opiates which merely suppress these ailments, presents one of our greatest social problems.

The problem is a dual one and both aspects of it are complementary. First, there is the need to give credence to the old truth,

9

despite all appearances in contemporary society, that the real satisfactions in life are not to be found in winning; or, if you can't win, by following other lines of less resistance. They are to be found by discovering and improving your own talents, wherever they may lie and however mediocre they may be, and by using some of them to help other people. Second, there is the need to gain effective recognition for the intrinsic merits of all those who, without the capacity for brilliance, take up the challenge of life with this outlook.

The Award Scheme is seen differently by different people, and rightly so. It is open for all young people of whatever abilities to take part, and to all adults to lend a hand. Some of the viewpoints, and especially the fun of 'having a go' and of helping young people to do so, are well put forward in David Wainwright's book. To do something because it is fun is as good a reason as any of many possible motives and for most kinds of activity. But the Scheme was offered mainly to convey not only a sense of enjoyment, but fulfil-ment to those who are affected by the social maladies of boredom and frustration; to help all who are concerned in dealing with this tremendous problem; who believe, despite the cynics, that a solution lies in positive adult leadership to evoke latent youthful enterprise; who accept the dictum of the Crowther Report that, even in those young people least blessed by circumstances, 'the challenge pro-duces the response'.

Youth in Action describes young people, typical of the great ordinary majority of their generation, discovering how to banish boredom, associate with adults, and make the most of life as they find it.

I have been very privileged to be associated with this new 'tool' for the service of youth, as Prince Philip has called it, ever since it was first sketched on the drawing board. The last eleven years in which it has been tested, modified and developed have been, for me, the most enthralling ones in my life.

15 December 1965

1 What the Scheme is about

A young electrician in Swindon, a secretary in Cardiff, a postman in Edinburgh, a schoolboy in London, a nurse in Durham, a handicapped cobbler in Lincolnshire, a shop assistant in Glasgow—all wear Prince Philip's badge. This means that they have made up their minds to achieve something, and then have gone ahead and done it. They have followed a programme with four sections, different in kind but linked in character.

They have travelled out of the towns and walked over the hills. They have performed some social service, by helping the old, the young or the sick. They have chosen one hobby and stuck to it for a set period of time. Finally, they are as fit as they can be.

The Duke of Edinburgh has called his scheme 'simply a challenge to the individual'.

'All he has to do is to achieve certain standards in subjects which he can choose himself in the four sections and he gets a certificate and a little badge to show it. Only if you have a go, you will find it is not quite as easy as all that!

The Scheme is based on a general assessment of present-day life. First of all, in education on the whole it is directed to passing exams, and only a relatively small number of schools have the inclination or the facilities to encourage extra-mural activities other than the traditional societies, clubs and organised team games, but as the Scheme is taken up in secondary schools, so, of course, their activities grow to take in the Scheme. Secondly, in a basically urban community it is not easy for the average parents to offer their children a wide choice of interesting activities. Thirdly—and most important to my mind—children and young people need an inducement to go out and try some new activity or interest, and until they have tried it they cannot know whether they are going to enjoy it or not. I may be wrong, but I suspect that much of the trouble young people get into is due to sheer boredom, because they have never had the chance to discover an absorbing interest. This Scheme is entirely practical and does not set out to preach in any way; in fact, the four sections of the Scheme are based on the average pattern of life outside working hours.

After all, there are very great numbers of people who devote a lot of time to some kind of voluntary public service or to service

13

of others. Most people also have some particular interest, sport or hobby which gives them pleasure and satisfaction. Then again, most people are more or less concerned about their physical well-being, even if it only amounts to avoiding illness and discomfort.

As to the expedition section, I can only say that every boy and girl with any gumption takes to the chance of a bit of adventure with enthusiasm. There is nothing like that wonderful feeling of having managed to achieve something which at one time seemed quite impossible, and this is an extremely pleasant way of doing it.

The Scheme is intended to help people to find out about the interesting and satisfying things in adult life. You do not have to join anything to start with; you do not have to belong to anything at the end. It can be used by any kind of youth organisation, school, club, firm or any kind of formal or informal body which has young people among its membership. In fact, it can be done entirely by individuals without any attachment whatsoever. Of course, it varies very much with each individual but, generally speaking, our experience is that gaining an Award brings with it a new sense of confidence and a wider outlook. . . .

For instance, in the public service and rescue training section, this suddenly brings home to people that they are really needed to help save life. Instead of being ordered out of the way because they are young and useless, they suddenly find themselves wanted and doing useful work alongside adults, friends and comrades.'[1]

In the ten years since the Duke of Edinburgh first issued his challenge to young people almost half a million boys and girls have taken it up. Of course, not all of them finish. But in the process most of them find wider interests, new excitements and a greater satisfaction than most would otherwise know in their daily lives. The results are not always obvious. No one can estimate how many lives have been transformed by the opportunities the Scheme has opened up. It must be a great many.

Not long ago Sir John Hunt, the Director of the Award Scheme, received a letter from a woman farming in a rural part of North

1. HRH the Duke of Edinburgh speaking to the Institute of Directors' conference, November 1962.

Wales. It reflects very well one of the changes the Scheme has brought about:

'Some few weeks ago I had car trouble. As I was alone, it necessitated a long six miles walk. *En route*, I passed three youngsters outside our nearest education recreation centre, standing by a little car. I explained my predicament. It was pouring with rain—and to cut a long story short, these three boys came up here, took off my tyre, took it to the village, repaired it, collected my spare, brought both up, and fitted them. All three, by then, were soaked.

I offered payment for petrol which was refused, so brought them in and warmed them. I was told all were up doing "Prince P.'s Gold Medal" from Birmingham. They were all three about 18, and all three hastily showed me the precious Silver Medal pinned to dirty T-shirts. With obvious pride, I was told every detail of what had to be accomplished, and how, and when, and that they all came up as often as they could, sometimes even just for a day, regardless of "Prince P." because they so loved this part of the world.

Finally I told them I was nearly always here, and if and when they and their friends came, officially or otherwise, they could always come. I again offered petrol money, and their only request was when they brought their girl friend could they bring her here, for tea, as it was "so lovely to be in a home—not a caff".

Yesterday a youngster of 18 arrived, with girl friend, Birmingham and Gold Medal, etc., and asked if he could ever come with a few friends and tent for weekends, and when not climbing could they help with walls, ditches, etc.

The point of all this is that HRH's Scheme has got them out of the cities, the factories, etc., into the countryside. It seems to me that many of these quite appalling-looking but completely sensible, reliable, adult-thinking youngsters long to get to places like this whenever they can, not just when they are officially Gold and Silver Medalling; it seems to me they want to help. . . .'

The writer of that letter went on to propose that she should offer two small cottages on her farm for the use of the young people taking part in the Scheme and their friends. The youngsters from

Birmingham had won her respect and affection, whatever they looked like.

They were no doubt ordinary young people. The Scheme demands nothing that cannot be achieved by the average boy or girl, in normal circumstances: it does not call for an extraordinary athletic performance. The Awards are intended for the ordinary young man and woman, and they have been won by schoolboys and schoolgirls in all types of school, including those for the handicapped; but also by young men and women who, having left school at 15 or 16, do the Scheme through youth clubs, pre-service units, factories, shops, offices and banks.

There are three standards of the Duke of Edinburgh's Award: Bronze, Silver and Gold. The Awards are given for the achievement of standards in certain specified activities, and may be attempted between certain ages. Boys and girls may attempt the Bronze standards between the ages of 14 and 16½, the Silver between the ages of 15 and 17½ and the Gold between 16 and 19 (though they may qualify for the Gold up to their 20th birthday).[1] In that time they will probably find that they have to devote one or two evenings each week, half a dozen weekends and from two to five days continuously (for an expedition) for each standard.

There is a tangible reward at the end of all this effort. For the Bronze, a certificate signed by Sir John Hunt (the Scheme's Director) and a bronze badge; for the Silver, a certificate signed by the Duke of Edinburgh, and a green and silver badge; and for the Gold, a certificate signed by the Duke of Edinburgh, a gold badge or brooch and an invitation to Buckingham Palace or Holyroodhouse, Edinburgh, with (for many) a handshake from the Duke.

But these rewards are negligible beside the rewards that many boys and girls have drawn from the Scheme—self-confidence, additional interests and an awareness of the countryside as a place for recreation and enjoyment. The numbers doing the Scheme are not great, but are increasing. At present, of the 5,000,000 boys and girls between the ages of 14 and 20 in Britain, one in every fifty starts the Scheme.

Only one in every 200 achieves even a Bronze Award, but this

1. The terms 'boys' and 'girls' are used here, and in the Scheme, for brevity. The young men and women who reach the Gold would probably prefer to be so described. Further details of the precise age limits are given at the back of this book.

Brian Wilson works as a window cleaner

Christine Leeds is a telephonist

Brian and Christine
learnt about the Scheme
from their local youth
service officer

As her 'interest'
Christine learnt to
play the guitar

As his 'interest' Brian took up photography

Brian passed his fitness tests
without difficulty

Christine took a course in party planning
and catering as part of the
Design for Living section

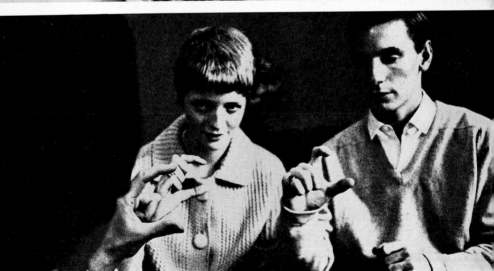

For their 'service' section
Brian and Christine studied the
deaf-and-dumb language

Christine lives in London, where there is
no shortage of interesting places to visit

With two friends, Brian set out on
a cross-country expedition

The end of a fascinating endeavour—
Brian and Christine receive their Silver Award certificates
from Sir John Hunt

is not necessarily because the Scheme's conditions are hard. More often it is because boys and girls find it difficult to carve out the time for the Scheme from the other demands made on that time at school or at work: and it is for them to say whether they are choosing to parcel out their time to the best advantage.

No doubt some are put off the Award Scheme because they have the wrong idea about it. Many people confuse it with Outward Bound,[1] and think that it means only that sort of concentrated physical endeavour. Other people associate the Award Scheme solely with mountaineering simply because the Director of the Scheme is Sir John Hunt, leader of the expedition that first climbed Everest in 1953. In fact, serious mountaineering is merely one option among more than 130 possible pursuits; it is quite possible to achieve a Gold Award without going anywhere near a mountain.

Another reason for confusion is the organisation of the Scheme. There is an Award Office in London, and others in Edinburgh, Cardiff and Belfast. But these Offices do not 'run' the Scheme: they provide information and advice. The people who run the Scheme are known as 'operating authorities'. These may be youth organisations, such as youth clubs, pre-service units, Scouts and Guides, the Boys' Brigade, etc.; or local education authorities, through their schools; or the armed forces and police forces. Some factories, offices, shops and banks also act as 'operating authorities'.

Throughout the country there are Award liaison officers, who voluntarily act as the representatives of the Award Office. So any boy or girl who does not know of a local 'operating authority' for the Scheme can be put in touch with one by the Award Office nearest to him or her. Of course, so loose a framework means that there are differences. The Scheme often takes the colour of the 'operating authority'; it tends to be run by the armed forces and the police as a more disciplined activity than it is, say, in youth clubs. Local Award Committees, on which the representatives of the different operating authorities sit, try to interpret the conditions and standards in a way that all can accept. But as there are thousands of approaches to life, so there are many ways of approaching the Scheme.

1. The main difference is that Outward Bound runs residential courses, lasting twenty-six days, at five schools in Britain. These schools, in the mountains or by the sea, mix young men and women from different backgrounds and, by putting them in physically testing situations, let them prove their endurance.

B

Once on a train I got into conversation with a young man who had been one of the first Gold Award winners, during the experimental phase of the Scheme, ten years ago. He assured me that it was tougher then, and that the youngsters doing it today were on a soft option. I supposed that his opinion was partly nostalgic, looking back from the craggy heights of his mid-twenties: but a few days later, talking to a group of schoolboys who assured me they were doing the Silver Award, I wondered. Because they let slip that they had been 'put in for' the Award by a schoolmaster, and it became clear that they had very little idea of what it was about. They couldn't say what they were doing for the Service section, and most of them were doing 'marksmanship' as a hobby. It seemed curious that all the boys in that form had chosen the same rather unusual hobby. But any good thing can be, and often is, distorted by someone, somewhere. I do not believe this 'volunteers—you, you and you' approach is typical of the way most young people start the Scheme.

How, then, does a boy or girl start? First, by finding an 'operating authority' to supervise the work. This does not mean that an Award candidate must be attached to any group or organisation: some 2,000 boys and girls have, in fact, completed the Scheme independently, during the past ten years. It takes additional persistence and initiative, and means that the candidate has often to nag adults until they help: but it can be done. It has been done, 2,000 times.

Then a Record Book has to be bought. This costs half a crown, is issued by the Award Office, and contains sections to be marked up at each stage until, with the final entry, the Gold is achieved. By the time the Record Book is handed to the candidate he will have decided what he is going to attempt for the Bronze.

The division of activity is equivalent for the Boys' and the Girls' Awards, but slanted differently. The main purpose is to offer young people opportunities for enjoyment and achievement. These are not the obvious forms of enjoyment, and yet there can hardly be a boy or girl who has gone through to the Gold who does not look back on the whole enterprise as a satisfying thing to have done. Most young people want to try themselves out, and the expeditions prove to them that they can walk longer distances and live less comfortably than they may have supposed. Most young people are eager to help less fortunate people if the opportunity is offered to them: and the public service section offers that opportunity. Most young people find it satisfying to reach defined standards of fitness. And while young people like to experiment with new interests and chase after the latest craze, many enjoy the sensation of pursuing one hobby, and sticking to it for a period, when there is a purpose behind this concentration.

These elements are built into the Award Scheme at each stage, Bronze, Silver and Gold. But they are put slightly differently for the boys and the girls. In each case there are four sections. Three are common to boys and girls—Service, Pursuits and Expeditions (though the girls call the last section Adventure). The fourth section for the boys is Physical Fitness, and for the girls Design for Living.

The purpose of the Service section is to remind young people that they are members of a community and have an obligation to others. This Service may involve taking a course leading to one of the certificates of the St John Ambulance Association, the British Red Cross Society or the St Andrew's Ambulance Association. In some districts courses are organised by the Fire Service, the Police and Civil Defence. Some of these courses—such as those in first aid—have an immediate and obvious practical value, particularly for the girls who take courses in nursing or child care.

For the Gold standard a candidate must do some form of practical service to the community, preferably for a period of six months. For this requirement many Gold Award winners have given remarkably selfless service in hospitals, homes for the disabled and handicapped, and in other forms of social work.

The Expedition is almost invariably the section of the Scheme that boys say they have enjoyed most. The expeditions are graded in difficulty: the Bronze expedition is little more than a long walk, while the Gold expedition must be done over four days, and fifty miles, in wild country—but always in groups of at least four, and after careful preparation and training.

Wild country is carefully defined for the purpose of the Gold expedition. The Award literature lists the areas in which Gold expeditions may be done as:

Dartmoor
Exmoor
Brecon Beacons and Black Mountains

Mid and North Welsh Mountains
The Peak District
The Isle of Man
The North Yorkshire Moors
The Lake District
The Pennines and Cheviots
The Sperrin Mountains and North Antrim Hills
Galloway Hills
Central Western and North Highlands of Scotland
Isles of Skye, Aran, Harris and Lewis

The requirements for the Gold expedition clearly state that most groups will be involved with journeys *through* mountainous country rather than over summit peaks. The expedition is a test of what the Duke of Edinburgh has called 'stickability'; it is not intended to be a tough and technical mountaineering exercise.

Beforehand, candidates must be properly trained to look after themselves, and the countryside; and, before they set out, qualified instructors must mark the Record Book to show that the boys have been trained. They must know the Casualty Code (an outline of elementary first aid, with special reference to emergencies in mountainous country), safety precautions, the use of map and compass, camp craft, cooking and the Country Code. All Award expeditions are supposed to be done between spring and autumn (though in Britain this is no guarantee of weather: one can sympathise with the young Glaswegian who put down his pack at the end of a soggy day in the Trossachs and announced that he wished the Duke of Edinburgh had never been born).

The Bronze expedition must cover at least fifteen miles across 'normal country', which is defined as agricultural, heath or common land, within a cycle or bus ride from most towns and cities. The journey must be completed in two days, including one night in tents or in the open. The Silver expedition demands thirty miles across rougher country unfamiliar to the candidates, including two nights at separate camp-sites. The Gold expedition calls for a march of at least fifty miles across wild country, during the four days and three nights of which the candidates must be dependent on themselves. The Silver and Gold expeditions may be carried out by bicycle, in canoes or boats, or skis, or on horseback—in which case the conditions vary from those given. For the Gold expedition the candidates must have the correct footwear and clothing, and carry navigational equipment and emergency rations.

The Adventure section for the girls is a less physically exhausting version of the Expedition section as done by the boys. For the Bronze, girls must complete a journey of six miles on foot or ten miles by cycle. For the Silver, the journey must take two days, with a night in a youth hostel or camping, and cover sixteen miles on foot or thirty miles by bike. For the Gold, the Adventure section expedition must take six days and five nights, and cover fifty miles on foot or 150 miles by bike, the candidates staying in youth hostels, climbing huts, tents or barns. The girls may pony-trek, or do their journey by canoe or sailing.

For the Gold, the girls have the alternative of a period of voluntary service with some 'worthwhile project', which is defined as 'helping on a farm, at a refugee centre abroad, in a children's holiday home or camp, at a National Union of Students' labour camp, with the Civic Trust, the Conservation Corps, an archaeological or similar project, or giving help through such organisations as International Voluntary Service'.

The Pursuits and Interests section is one of the most fascinating aspects of the Scheme. The handbook for the Boys' Award lists 130 pursuits from aero-modelling, through choirs (Roman Catholic) and music (military flautists) to zoology, and the Girls' Awards list even more possible interests, such as knitting and soft-toy making. Any young man or woman who cannot find a hobby in these pages must be dull indeed. The idea of this section is to encourage boys and girls to discover and develop their talents by taking up a particular hobby or interest and sticking to it for six months (for the Bronze and Silver) or a year (for the Gold). Though the handbook syllabuses have been worked out by recognised authorities (those on architecture, for example, have been drafted by the Royal Institute of British Architects), they are not exam syllabuses—young people have enough exams in their lives. Because the people who act as tutors for these various interests may not know what sort of standards to apply the handbooks are intended as a guide only. This section is broadened by the inclusion of various sports—archery, boxing, gymnastics, judo, wrestling—which can be taken as Pursuits or Interests.

However, all boys must, as the fourth section of the Scheme, reach certain standards of physical fitness. For example, for the Bronze a boy must run 100 yards in 13 seconds, for the Silver 100 yards in 12·2 seconds and for the Gold 100 yards in 11·8 seconds. For the Bronze and Silver he must reach standards in any three of five groups: running or walking, jumping, throwing, swimming or physical efficiency. The handicapped are judged by special panels, each of which usually has a doctor member.

In place of the Physical Fitness section the girls complete a course called Design for Living. Most girls after leaving school go out and work for a time, earning wages and living independently. The Design for Living section encourages girls to have the widest general interests during that period of independence, but also to have the chance of finding out more about the technical details of starting and running a home. This section is divided into three groups, with a choice from among 18 activities. For the Bronze a girl must follow one activity, together with the syllabus on good manners. For the Silver a second activity is chosen. For the Gold, two activities are followed, or one pursued for a longer period. Of the three groups of activities, the first is called Grooming and Poise, in which girls can learn the secrets of make-up and hair styles, dress sense, and entertaining. The second group is called Setting Up Your Home, and includes information on how to get a mortgage and buy or rent a house, personal and home budgeting, and such practical details as the care and use of electrical equipment.

The third group in the Design for Living section is Running Your Home, which introduces the prospective housewife to cleaning and repairing, planning meals for the family, gardening and floral decoration. For girls over 17 there is an extra, optional choice— The Girl, the Boy, and Marriage.

In addition, for the Gold, boys and girls must live away from home for a period—possibly on a training course, or in some form of voluntary service. This residential qualification is planned as proof for everyone (including the candidates themselves) that they are capable of living even for a short period in a community other than their own home—in other words, to show that they can get on with other people.

In Arnold Wesker's play *Roots* Beatie Bryant makes a protest against the apathy, complacency and laziness of her family:

'Oh yes, we turn on a radio or a TV set maybe, or we go to the pictures—if them's love stories or gangsters—but isn't that the easiest way out? Anything so long as we don't have to make an effort. . . . Education ent only books and music—it's asking questions, all the time. There are millions of us, all over the country, and no one, not one of us is asking questions.'

There are today many thousands of young people tramping across Dartmoor, Wales, the Peak District or the Scottish hills who first went there on foot through the Scheme. There are many more who are nurses or youth-club workers or apprentices because the opportunities were shown to them through the Scheme.

The Award winners are not a conformist lot. They have made an effort, and they are question-asking people: highly critical, articulate, intelligent and argumentative. For them the Scheme has opened doors on life that might otherwise have remained closed, leaving them in the dark house of boredom.

2 How the Scheme works

Four young men from Birmingham are tramping across Snowdonia in the rain. Each has a 30 lb pack of equipment, and they pause from time to time to take a compass bearing. They talk about the weather, their own idiocy (as it seems in that moment) in starting the Scheme in the first place and the prospects of reaching the rendezvous previously agreed with their instructor. They march on; and one optimist says—as the rain drips down his neck and he skids on the wet moss—'One day we'll laugh about this, I suppose.'

And they will. Even the most uncomfortable expedition takes on a certain glamour in retrospect. After all, their expedition was that much stiffer than other people's. And they did it. Even though the climate conspired against them they got through the course. Back in Aston and Sparkbrook and Edgbaston they will remember: and having sworn that never again will they set foot on the Welsh hills, one will say to another, 'Next weekend, why don't we . . .?' and on the Friday evening they will be on Crewe station *en route* for Llangollen. Possibly with the girl friend.

Many of their colleagues are luckier with the weather. The expedition is a very popular part of the Scheme, and though some young men find the preparations—the map-reading, Casualty Code, the emphasis on safety—a bit tedious, all enjoy the expedition.

The preparations are essential to it. The Scheme's organisers do not ask that the young people shall do hazardous things on this venture. Indeed the whole point of careful preparation is that the more dangerous risks are taken out of the expedition. Each member must know what to do if one of his friends slips on wet rocks and breaks a limb, what to do if mist comes unexpectedly down on the hills, what to do if someone is taken suddenly ill. There have been accidents on Award expeditions, but such things are the very rare exception.

Who are these young men and women? Last weekend they could quite easily have been at the coast on their motor-bikes. They are no different from the great majority of their friends, except for the one essential difference—they have found ways of getting the most out of their leisure time. Not expensive or destructive pleasures, but the joy of walking through the country with no sound but birdsong and the chat of friends—and the satisfaction of knowing that beyond the next ridge is a camp-site and a rest: knowing this because they have worked it out on a map, planned it beforehand and have confidence in their own planning. They might even (which would astonish Mum if she realised) set to and cook a simple and satisfying meal.

The Scheme's activities fall so naturally into place in the lives of thousands of young people that they are accepted as ordinary. Few of those who take part stop to think what they would be doing if they were not doing this. Some would be working for exams, others would be propping up the counter of the coffee-bar, one or two might be breaking up some seaside town for kicks. The game of 'what might have been' is a fruitless one, and the Scheme is not a system of reform.

But if we accept that much of the destructive element among young people is caused by a lack of anything better to do, then the Scheme is an answer: because it offers so many better things to do. Not in those terms, though. Who would willingly take up any activity because someone else said, 'This is better for you than what you're doing now'? No: the youngsters would be weak-willed indeed if they agreed.

In North London there is a youth club in a tough area. Its members come from many parts of London. It is one of the clubs started on the initiative of the Duke of Edinburgh, and not surprisingly some of the members do the Scheme. They do it because they choose to do it—which is the reason they join the club in the first place. One evening I was standing by the club coffee-bar with the club leader when three small boys of about thirteen came up. They wanted to buy NABC badges and become members. No one had told them to join. Their friends belonged, enjoyed the club, and made others want to join of their own free will.

'In a club like this I don't think there will ever be more than eight or ten boys doing the Scheme,' said the club leader. 'I don't think there should be. They've got to want to do it. They've got to come along and make the effort to find out about it. But they do.'

There is nothing soft about the members of that club. One popular club activity is judo. But they also make films. And the club runs a Social Service Squad. There is a good deal of competition to belong to it. Usually there are only eight members, and most of them are using it to qualify for the Service section of the Scheme.

On Monday evenings they take the club bus, collect mentally handicapped children from the district, take them to their own

club and spend the evening talking and playing with them. One or
two of the boys are learning sign language so that they can talk to
deaf-and-dumb children. These are tough young men: they are
also involved in a number of different activities, all purposeful,
and some of them with the additional point that they qualify
towards achieving the Silver or the Gold. These young men are
printers' apprentices, builders' labourers, clerks. They start giving
their time to backward children under the challenge of the Scheme:
they go on doing so because they find satisfaction in it.

Today many young men and women start the Scheme at school,
then continue it at a youth club or with some other youth organisation. Colin, for example, was introduced to it at the Morrison
Boys' School, Liverpool. Thanks largely to Ronald Deadman, the
teacher who administered it, the Scheme got outstanding results at
Morrison.

Those who say that the Scheme is 'easier' for schools have some
evidence for their arguments at Morrison, where even the expeditions
are planned in relation to the school curriculum. Candidates for
the Gold are given a week off school at the end of the spring term,
ferried across to the Isle of Man and set to their map-reading and
planning. When the Golds finish and are on their way back from
Douglas they meet the Silver and Bronze groups on their way out.
Each year there are some twenty-five Bronze candidates from
Morrison, twenty Silver and a dozen or so Gold.

So Colin 'did his Bronze' in a group of twenty-five, without
thinking a great deal about it. For 'service' he took his first-aid
certificate, for 'pursuit' he read various recommended books—
including some popular books on mathematics—and for 'fitness'
he passed some swimming tests and the standard for the three-mile
road walk.

At Easter 1961, with his contemporaries from Morrison who
were all doing the Bronze stage, he went to the Isle of Man. They
hiked across the Isle of Man in the rain, in platoons of six. When
the rain eased they taught themselves how to light a fire, and how
to heat up the inevitable stew (though that came out of tins). They
carefully wrote up their logs, making the required 'observations'
of churches and other buildings along the route. And they reached
the right place at the right time, and qualified for the Bronze,

though the Isle of Man Award examiner, Frank Coven, noted acidly on Colin's log that he need not have explained how difficult it had been to wash greasy dishes in the cold water of a stream. You might try heating some water, said the examiner. It hadn't occurred to them, being city boys away from home for the first time, that hot water would have done the job better.

The Bronze Awards were presented, with some small ceremony, in Morrison school hall. At that time there was no great natural enthusiasm among the boys for going on with the Scheme, but Mr Deadman wasn't having any backsliding. They would do the Silver, and like it.

At Garston Baths they qualified for the Royal Life Saving Certificate. Yet again Colin did his eighteen circuits of the school track, this time within the standard for the Silver Award. He even tackled throwing the cricket ball. 'It took about an hour,' he says in retrospect. 'The furthest I could get, at the start, was 100 ft; but I got to 175 ft 10 in. before my arm fell off. . . .' With some other athletic tests, he was up to the fitness standard.

For the 'pursuit' qualification he chose popular music. His English master, David R. Dixson, was himself a capable jazz musician playing in a Liverpool group; and Colin made a detailed study of the current pops which he then presented to, and was examined by, Mr Dixson. 'I had to analyse the reasons for the success of Elvis Presley, and that sort of thing.'

The Morrison Silver expedition travelled to the Isle of Man at Easter 1962. There were thirty of them, divided into patrols of six. It was another wet Easter and the rain came down continuously for two days. The patrols planned their own routes and chose their own camps from the maps; these were then checked off beforehand by the examiners, who periodically visited the expeditions to make sure they were still on the right routes. Colin's group chose to camp at Ballaragh and Sulby Glen; and as the three days wore on they became more and more weary.

Once, coming to the edge of a valley lined with gorse bushes, with a river at the bottom, they took a deep breath and battered their way down through the gorse and across the wide, but fortunately shallow, river. Pausing on the other side to let the water out of their boots (which then became practically impossible to put on again), they looked back to find that they had been scratching their way down through the gorse within 100 yards of a quite clear open path down the hill; and that just round the escarpment there was a small but adequate bridge over the river. From that time on they read their maps meticulously before making any rash move.

In the year that followed, Colin was taking his GCE 'O' Levels; but somehow 'taking the Award' had become almost second nature, and it seemed reasonable to go ahead and attempt the Gold. At Garston Baths he achieved the Award of Merit of the Royal Life Saving Society. On the school track he yet again did his eighteen circuits, for the last time, to qualify for the three-mile walk—and added to it standards for the long jump, shuttle relay and spring.

At Easter 1963 the twelve 'Gold candidates' from Morrison went across to the Isle of Man yet again. The expedition, done in platoons of four, was much tougher. They began at Eary Cushlin, a remote National Trust house a mile away from any farm, high on the moors; and with camps at Glenneedle, Glen Crammag and Inglebreck they made their way down to Ramsay. This expedition involved much rougher country than the Bronze and Silver, with climbs up to and down from peaks of 2,000 ft.

Back in Liverpool, Colin was spending two nights a week at the Domestic Mission Youth Club near his home at Park Place—helping with the administration, organising activities and supervising games. The Club is a member of the 50,000-strong Liverpool Boys' Association, and rather to his astonishment (he claims because there was no one else who would volunteer) Colin was elected chairman of the Members Council of the Liverpool Boys' Association for 1963–4.

An average of twenty-five member-representatives met monthly at the LBA headquarters in Shiel Road, and discussed all aspects of youth-club activities, from the organisation of cricket, football and boxing competitions to the use of the Association's Heswall camp and general philosophical questions about the best way to run a youth club. The points raised would then be discussed with a comparable council of youth leaders.

On one occasion, Colin, as chairman, received the LBA's annual cheque from the Liverpool United Voluntary Organisations. 'That was a day—I was walking round Liverpool with a cheque for £3,000 in my pocket.'

As another part of his 'service' requirement for the Gold Award,

Colin was visiting some old people who lived alone; but he did not
find that the ones he was recommended to see (by the local Council
of Social Service) very much wanted his visits. 'I went to see one
old dear and she started on about the rent. She went on about the
rent for about half an hour. Then I said I hadn't come about the
rent, I'd come to visit her, and she said, oh, her grand-daughter
came to visit her, thanks very much, and she didn't want any
more visitors.'

As his 'pursuit' for the Gold, Colin decided to continue with his
study of pop music and jazz. His particular specialisation was the
banjo, its history and its place in pop music. 'One of the masters
at Morrison was Selwyn Cash—he'd been a great banjo player in
the thirties, on radio and all that, and he gave me a lot of information.'

Meanwhile Colin was teaching himself the guitar. So were most
of the other 16-year-olds in Liverpool, for this was the beginning
of the great Liverpool beat-group boom. He had also gone as far
as he could go at Morrison School and was transferred to the
sixth form at one of the Liverpool grammar schools, Quarry Bank
(where, he was pleased to note, Paul McCartney had been a pupil).

He was still spending two nights a week at the Domestic Mission,
and began to set up a small guitar school there—a few of the boys
who had earlier formed their own group which, in the way of these
Liverpool groups, had then split and re-formed and split again. It
was shortly after he went to Quarry Bank that Colin Lomas had
confirmation that he had achieved the Gold Award. There was no
presentation at Quarry Bank: he was handed the white-and-gold
lapel badge, with Prince Philip's cipher, casually in a corridor.
(Was it between a physics and a maths period? He can't remember.)

In July 1964 Colin went to one of the twice-yearly receptions at
Buckingham Palace and was one of the lucky few, out of the
900-odd boys and girls present, to whom Prince Philip spoke.

The Scheme now has a place in all types of school. Woodberry
Down was the first mixed comprehensive school opened (in 1955)
by the London County Council: now it educates more than a
thousand pupils from the Stoke Newington area of North London.
This vast school, with boys and girls between the ages of 11 and
18, with all grades of scholarship and all shades of interest, throbs
with life.

The boys and girls of Woodberry Down who do the Scheme in their spare time are all volunteers. Usually about thirty each year start to work for the Bronze: perhaps a dozen stick at it and achieve the Bronze, half a dozen go on to the Silver, and one, two or three each year manage to get the Gold.

They choose many different pursuits. Robert, who is 17, a school prefect and house captain, is a cool, calm and amiable person who became interested in stage lighting for the slightly quixotic reason that 'in theatre programmes you see the names of the actors, and the producers, but not often the name of the chap who did the lighting—and I want to put that right'.

He was astonished, when he first took up the Scheme, to discover that he could use his interest in stage lighting as his 'pursuit'—and so he went on with it until he became master of the Woodberry Down lighting console and the lighting expert for several of the amateur theatrical groups in the neighbourhood.

Robert was also keen on aeronautics and had taken an RAF selection test. There, he found, his experience in the various activities of the Scheme was immeasurably valuable. 'Basically, it's the business of learning to look after yourself,' he says. 'Quite apart from the skills like map-reading and first aid, which are useful, it's satisfying to be doing things you'd not otherwise be doing—such as camping, and walking.'

Robert had reached his Silver standard: one of his contemporaries, Jimmy, had reached the Gold. He agreed with Robert that the greatest satisfaction he had found was the broadening of his interests. 'I used to go on holiday with the family to Scotland, but I'd never have thought of walking anywhere—I'd never have thought I'd enjoy it. But now I do enjoy it, and I'm sure I shall go on doing it.'

Jimmy is an engineer, who will probably take a student apprenticeship or a Higher National Certificate when he leaves school. For his pursuit he chose 'citizenship', examining the structure of local government and the history of the constitution. He appreciates the irony of the fact that lower down the school he hated history, and learnt to enjoy it when he was studying it out of school.

He remembers, also with some irony, what made him join in the Scheme in the first place. 'It was in the school hall one day, when I was small, and some of the older boys went up to get their gold

c

badges. It was hero-worship, in a way: it seemed such a wonderful achievement. When I went up to get my own Gold badge it all seemed very ordinary.

'You can't really blame the people who don't go on to the Gold,' he continued. 'It's very difficult to carry on with it in a year when you're also taking "A" Levels. And the Gold isn't easy—I found the fitness tests very tough—it took me two years to pass them.

'I think the Gold expedition could be tougher. But that may be because it was tougher for me than it has been for some of my friends. I took it up in the Peak District, with the Boys' Brigade, and that was a very tough expedition indeed, in country where the land is never level for more than a hundred yards in any direction so that you're going up and down all the time, and the ground's spongy when it's level.'

The other section of his Gold work that has already proved useful to Jimmy in a slightly perverse way is the first aid. Just after reaching Gold standard he dislocated his shoulder playing rugby. He couldn't very well set the shoulder but he made an immediate correct and furious diagnosis.

'I suppose,' said the Headmistress of the Penge County Secondary School for Girls, with a twinkle in her eye, 'all my girls will now be going mountaineering!' She knew, really, that the Scheme was more than mountaineering, but her half-humorous remark showed that in her mind she associated even the Girls' Award with outdoor activities. She had reason to be slightly put out: her after-school telephoning had been deafened by the sound of half a dozen boys and thirty girls dancing a 'Mod march' down the corridor outside her room.

Mrs Peggy Spencer, the famous ballroom-dancing teacher, had been conducting an after-school class. Some of the boys from the associated boys' county school had come in as partners. For four of the girls the dancing class was more than just a pleasant activity. They had chosen ballroom dancing as their 'pursuit' for the Bronze standard of the Scheme, and at the end of the term Mrs Spencer would be testing them to see that they had reached the necessary skill.

The Scheme had only recently been started at this school—because of the arrival of a teacher, Mrs Penlington, who had been involved in it at her last school. She had suggested the idea to some of the girls, rightly insisting that only volunteers should do the Scheme, that they should do it out of school time and that the numbers taking part would be limited.

At this school the running of the Scheme was still at the planning stage. Mrs Penlington explained that as part of the Design for Living section, which is a requirement of the Girls' Scheme, there were to be classes on safety in the home.

Gillian, who is 14, said, 'I didn't have many hobbies before, so I thought this would be a way of making some.' She was a little apprehensive of the expedition, but she had been for long walks with the school's Christian Union and no doubt would enjoy the walking (which is the main part) of the girls' expedition. Marilyn, a pretty dark girl, said that she had heard of the Award before it started at the school, but she didn't know much about it and no one had suggested before that she might go in for it.

But these two, and their friends, were enjoying the opportunities that the Scheme was offering them to widen their interests; and they were particularly lucky to be in one of the seventeen dancing classes conducted in the schools of South London by Mrs Spencer. 'Some of the girls think when they start that they were just born to dance,' she said. 'And then they find that they have to apply them-selves to learning the proper steps. But most of them are very enthusiastic and they learn quickly.'

Most of them realise that they will get much more fun out of going dancing if they really know the steps, instead of being condemned just to shuffling round the dance floor.

Mrs Peggy Spencer has been aware of the Award Scheme almost since it started, for she was one of those involved in preparing the schedule of standards for ballroom dancing, approved by the Imperial Society of Teachers of Dancing and published in the official handbook of pursuits and projects.

But it is surprising to find that (perhaps because of the smaller number of girls taking the Scheme) all the Award candidates that Mrs Spencer has tested in the classes at her own dancing school at the Royston Ballroom and its Orpington branch have been boys. One young man carried on with dancing as his hobby, and having completed the tests within the Award Scheme went on to achieve a Bronze Medal of the Imperial Society, yet another instance of someone starting a hobby as part of the Scheme and continuing with it to reach the highest standards in the adult world.

In a room behind the pillared portico of Sir Walter Scott's foundation in Edinburgh's New Town a group of young gentlemen —formidably clean, well groomed and self-assured—stood politely behind their desks. A typical cross-section of the polite public schoolboys, anonymous in the cerulean blue blazers of the Edinburgh Academy: a scholar, an athlete, a prospective architect, lawyer, doctor, business man. Yet of the nine, one wore a Gold badge, four a Silver, two a Bronze.

Alasdair, from Oban, bespectacled and articulate, taking 'A' Levels that summer in maths and physics, then probably going on to a university to study architecture or engineering. He was the Gold winner, and produced photographs of the models he had made for his 'pursuit'. They were detailed, delicate and complex models of bridges, produced from his own scaled plans. As his 'public service' he had helped at the Cheshire Homes for the disabled in Edinburgh.

Beside him, Peter, stocky and fair, likely to achieve his Gold this summer—and become the third (and last) brother in a family of Gold Award winners. His eldest brother, John, is now a second lieutenant in the Royal Engineers: his second brother, Andrew, is reading medicine at Oxford. Peter's 'pursuit' has been highland dancing. He is a boarder at Edinburgh, and his family is in Pakistan where his father has a business. He himself hopes to become a vet, and wants to work in New Zealand.

Third of the Academy boys, Alan, will probably go into the law. His 'pursuit' was reading, and he produced a formidable seventeen-page critique of the *Seven Pillars of Wisdom* which he had read to attain Gold standard.

They were all polite and informative; but then they produced a geographical model of the Trossachs, and in concert described their Gold Award expedition. They had all said, as every boy says, that the bit of the Scheme they had enjoyed most was the expedition: and now, describing the route and the hazards of a wet week in March, they proved it with a stream of reminiscence shared between the scholar, the athlete and the lawyer.

They had walked along Loch Striven to the first camp-site in

Glen Massen, where early on their expedition they were flooded out. Along Loch Eck to their second camp, ten miles on: then a climb of 2,000 ft to Loch Goil and Loch Long. There it was very wet indeed, and they slept in a barn. At this point on the map one of them had written: 'Eureka! The sun came out!' as they trudged down through Glen Fyne to Ben Bhuidhe.

It was, from the sound of it, the sort of expedition that is much more delightful in retrospect than at the time. I was reminded of the story of another Academy boy, a younger one new to map-reading, who was sent out on a short trial expedition with some of his friends. He had been given, in error, an HM Ordnance Survey map that was forty years old, and did not show a reservoir subsequently built. Coming upon this sheet of water, the boys misread the map and trudged ten miles out of their way before they were rescued by a master who said to them:

'Prince Philip wouldn't think much of your standard of map-reading.'

'Well, sir,' said the boy, 'and I don't think much of the standard of his wife's maps.'

Later that evening I went down to the Canongate youth club, at the gates of Holyrood Palace. There the two worlds came together, for I found four Silver Award winners. One, John, from Edinburgh Academy, was helping at the club as his service towards the Gold Award, which he would probably reach during 1965—at the same time as he was taking a group of Highers and 'A' Levels, academically, at the Academy. Broad of frame and gently spoken, he talked about his taking the Award and said, very frankly, that he felt that it had been much easier for him than for the boys at the Club. So he went down to help two youngsters, Billy and Andy, dour young Scots, who were due to do a first-aid test for their Bronze.

After this 'Accie' it was a contrast—but not so great a contrast as all that—to meet three other Silver Award winners. The only thing that obviously differentiated them, perhaps, was that John was in the blue blazer of the Academy, while Ronald, James and David were wearing the smart clothes of young men at work. Ronald is a postman, David a clerical assistant in the Post Office and James is a glass-blower.

They told me about their Silver expedition into the Lammer-muirs, and also about their various pursuits—Ronald as a boy taking the Bronze had made a collection of match-boxes: James had blown a glass swan. But their main distinction was that with a fourth colleague, David, they had made a study of the National Savings Movement, its purpose and organisation, so thorough that the Chairman of the Local Savings Committee, Sir Ian Johnson-Gilbert, himself supervised the Award.

Some of the pursuits and interests done within the framework of the Scheme are highly technical and demand great concentration. This confirms the Scheme's success in providing a stimulus for activity, rather than yet another exam. For many boys and girls achieve a very professional and adult standard in their hobbies.

On the wall of the bedroom at the top of a South Kensington house is suspended an accurate line drawing of a seventy-four-gun sailing ship. The drawing is stretched on a system of jumbo clips, cords and weights, so that the clips tauten the plan without tearing it, but so that the plan can be replaced with another from the roll stored on the top of the cupboard.

The plans and elevations are of a naval ship of about 1813, the last of the classical 'wooden walls'. In the shed at the bottom of the garden Francis is building a model, to the precise scale of three-sixteenths of an inch to the foot, which makes the final model something over two feet long. So far he has completed two of the three skins of the hull, first sculpting a keel of marine plywood, measuring out with precise accuracy the bulkheads and deck supports. The first skin is of plates of plywood laid vertically, the second of broader planks laid horizontally, and the third to be of scaled-down planks curving round the hull.

The model has so far taken many Sundays throughout almost three years, and may take those others that Francis can spare while reading for a university exam in his subject, modern languages. The idea of building the model came from one of his elder brothers, who bought the plans (from Harold A. Underhill of Glasgow). But now Francis talks the technicalities of the navy of the Napoleonic wars, and expounds vigorously the details of the orlop-deck, the procedures for clearing for action, the exact methods of securing, manœuvring, loading and firing the guns: thirty-two-pounders on the lower deck, eighteen-pounders and carronades on the upper.

'I decided when I started to build the thing that it was going to float,' he says—and keeps on another wall, as a reminder perhaps, an elevation of the classical Swedish sailing-ship *Vasa*, which sank on its launching. The guns, too, may fire. 'One must defend oneself against aggressive swans,' is Francis's comment, with tongue in cheek. He plans to make the cannon from brass tubing, wound with wire and then cast in lead: he toys with the idea of firing them electrically, with ten caps to a gun, which will no doubt surprise the other boatmen on the Round Pond or wherever this ship makes its maiden voyage.

Her name is still undecided. She may be called after one of the ships actually built from plans such as these, at Chatham Dockyard in or about 1813—*Wellesley, Redoubtable, Cornwallis, Melville* or *Black Prince*. Or she may be called *Unicorn:* and Francis will carve an appropriate figurehead.

With some people this sort of pursuit could obviously become an obsession—the collection of books, papers and pictures on the ships of the Napoleonic wars, culminating in a scale model of one of them. But across the bed lay a pair of pseudo-Elizabethan rapiers— made by Francis. 'They're doing *Henry IV*, Part I, at school, and they got me in to help with the rapier and dagger fight with Hal and Hotspur—so we decided we'd better have the proper things.'

Understandably, the pursuits chosen by boys at a school such as Francis's—Westminster—are esoteric. Building a seventy-two-gun sailing-ship is almost conventional. His contemporaries are doing projects on the King Pawn openings in chess; methods of confining wild animals in the twentieth century; London's city churches; the temples of Kanah and Luxor; and telepathy. Among other things.

At Westminster the Scheme is an alternative to the Corps. There are usually about twenty participating in any year, and they are elected by a self-electing committee of five.

For public service (since few go beyond the Silver stage) some do a first-aid course conducted by one of the school doctors, and others have joined in a police course organised at Rochester Row police station. Others have spent weekends helping to clear the churchyard at Newport Pagnell. Bronze expeditions have been done on Corps field days: Gold and Silver expeditions have been organised in Ireland, Wales and Scotland.

Francis would, he agreed, no doubt have built the ship in any case, Award or no Award—though the Scheme had given the project a framework and an immediate purpose, as well as a small slot in his personal and extremely congested time-table. 'It's a great thing,' he says, 'just to get away from books now and then, and concentrate on something so entirely different.' Which is as good a definition of the full use of leisure as you could wish to find.

But technical projects are not limited to the public schools. One group of Award candidates runs a radio station.

You can't get Radio St Athan on any radio set. Reception is limited to the barrack-room of the Royal Air Force station at St Athan in Glamorgan (which is probably best known as the base for a famous mountain rescue unit, and other rescue services on that rough coast). On that station there is a Boy Entrants' unit, which takes in boys straight from school and gives them an eighteen-month course before they are posted to other units as regular servicemen in the Royal Air Force.

Any boys' unit in the services is well placed to do the Award Scheme. The boys are under military discipline, so they soon learn not to get bored with the tasks they undertake—boredom is actively discouraged in the services. There is the further stimulus that life in the services is a 'closed society', in which people must necessarily learn to live together in groups almost for twenty-four hours of the day, seven days a week. All boys' units have to face the problem of what to do with the boys in the evenings, for technical training cannot go on from dawn to dusk, and yet the boys remain under discipline in the camp.

For such units the Scheme has proved a great attraction both to the officers and to the boys. The officers find that the Scheme suggests a great many out-of-hours activities which in the old days they had to invent in order to keep the boys busy: and for the boys themselves the Award Scheme represents something outside the daily routine, which takes them outside the camp for many of its training sessions, and which is thus a link with the civilian world outside.

So the problem at St Athan, as in many other similar units in the RAF, the Army and the Navy, is that if anything there are too many candidates presenting themselves for Award courses. As anywhere else, all candidates must be volunteers: but the number volunteering is almost 100 per cent, out of a spontaneous feeling among the boys that the Scheme is 'something different' from the services routine. At St Athan there are on average about 160 boys in each annual intake, of whom about one-tenth bring with them record books proving that they have already been taking part in the Scheme at school (and as most boys come from secondary modern schools this confirms the general view that the Scheme is now being used extensively for the 'final year' in those schools). Of the sixteen or so who hold record books, usually between six and ten have already reached the Bronze Award. Occasionally a 16-year-old might have the Silver: and there was one famous day when one boy arrived as a fully paid-up holder of the Gold.[1]

A boys' unit in the services is also well placed to do the Award Scheme because so many of its requirements are available on a services station. First aid, for example, is part of the boys' normal course. They learn elementary map-reading within the syllabus of their ground-combat training, and they have no problems when it comes to kitting themselves out for expeditions. The RAF Physical Training School at St Athan has plenty of sports facilities, even including canoes which the boys can borrow: some boys as their 'pursuit' go canoeing on the Wye. The aspects of service—Fire Service, Civil Defence rescue, and life saving—are also of immediate use in forces training. But at St Athan, as in other similar units, the boys taking the Award must do their training and be tested for these sections in their spare time.

Many boys join the RAF because they are interested in aircraft: so there is a popular demand for aero-modelling and aircraft recognition as 'pursuits'. The boys' unit also has a band; and also its own magazine, edited and produced by the boys themselves. And there is Radio St Athan.

A Senior Boy Entrant, Bob, from Catterick Camp in Yorkshire, is one of those who helps to man and run the radio station which does live broadcasts from 6 pm until Lights Out at 9.30 pm, interspersed with recorded tapes and Radio Luxembourg. Bob said he had enjoyed most parts of the Scheme, especially the expedition—even though their expedition went on for longer than most, because

1. Until 1965 it was theoretically possible for a boy to obtain the Gold at the 'beginning of the age-scale for it, if he could reach the necessary standards'. Now the conditions state that he must have followed his chosen 'pursuit' for at least twelve months from the date he began the Gold course—and as he cannot begin until he is 16 he cannot reach Gold Award standard before he is 17.

one group was caught in the mist on the last day and walked several miles out of its way.

But Radio St Athan was his great enthusiasm. He showed me round the hut, divided into two studios, a control room, tape room, record library and editing room, and coiled his length into the controller's chair to demonstrate the highly professional deck with its amplifiers, turntables and suspended microphones. Apart from running the technical side of the radio station, the boy entrants prepare their own programmes: and Bob found that the index of pop discs he compiled from the *New Musical Express* as the log of his 'pursuit' was coming in useful as a day-to-day source of reference in making up programmes for the radio.

No doubt this, too, will become part of his life in the RAF, though what he puts over on the radio will probably not be pop music. Quiet and reticent, he turned knobs and twiddled dials as if it were second nature, and came to life when seated in the midst of so much highly technical equipment. And that, in itself, is one of the things the Scheme was started to encourage: concentration.

3 Part of the community

Most young people want to belong. They want to belong to their own groups, and to the adult world. But too often the adult world will not accept their terms, and then they become 'delinquents' and are caught and punished, or merely become 'unclubbable', people who will not accept the restrictions of society.

And should they? Are all society's rules desirable? Every young man or young woman questions the rules his elders have lived by. Some later accept them and become responsible members of society. Others go on questioning, and sometimes carry their questions into action. When that action becomes anti-social they find themselves in court.

The Scheme is not a means of reforming the wild ones. Nor is it intended to be a way of making them conform to any predestined pattern. It offers a hundred opportunities of self-discovery and fulfilment; and one of the most satisfying results is the effect its introduction has had in places where the young often feel themselves cornered, defensive and defeated—the approved schools.

The following story is entirely true. Only the name of the young man concerned, and those of some of the places, have been changed. Call him Jim.

Jim lived in an industrial town in the north-east. He was 16, working as a builder's labourer, and taking home £4 10s a week. He kept £1 of that as spending money, and his mother used to bank another 10s for him and let him have it when he wanted to buy clothes, which he often did. School, for Jim, had been a running battle with authority. His teachers thought him sly, difficult and lazy. I don't know what he thought of them.

His father had a good job in a factory, but often worked on the night shift. His mother too, went out working in the evenings, so that Jim often had the house to himself and could ask his friends round to sample his father's drinks—until his father locked them away. There was plenty of money in the house—but not much home life.

That summer, as the family holiday in Blackpool approached, Jim's father discovered that the boy had saved nothing towards it, and so stopped his pocket money. Suddenly Jim, alone among his friends, had no money in his pocket. One day he was in a shop when the assistant went into the back, leaving the till open. Jim extracted some money: the theft was traced to him, and he appeared in the juvenile court. A little later he ganged up with three friends and broke and entered another shop, and stole some more money. This time, he was committed to an approved school.

Jim told the people who interviewed him then that he would like to go to sea. So he was sent to the Wellesley Nautical School, an approved school run on naval disciplinary lines, from which about half the boys go to sea—with the Royal or Merchant Navies, or as fisher boys.

As a new entrant, Jim was told about the Award Scheme. It was explained to him that while at Wellesley, in addition to the school classes he would attend, he would be able to choose certain hobbies or pursuits that he could do during the winter months.

For the boys at Wellesley this offered the advantage of seeing new faces from 'outside' and even, for some of the classes in 'public service', going into the neighbouring town of Blyth where classes in firemanship were held in the fire station, and civil defence at the CD headquarters.

Jim chose to attend the first-aid classes given at the school by George Henderson, the divisional superintendent of the St John Ambulance Brigade in Blyth. Mr Henderson is a retired miner's deputy overman who has made the St John Ambulance work his great interest. He soon communicated his enthusiasm to Jim, who within four months had passed his preliminary St John's first-aid exam.

With a friend, Roy, whom he had met at the school, Jim teamed up for St John's work. There is always a shortage of volunteers for such work, and soon Jim and his colleague were in demand for first-aid posts.

They were so keen, and so efficient, that they were appointed auxiliaries in the Blyth Brigade. During the summer there was a St John's first-aid post on the beach, and for much of the time the two boys—on special passes from the approved school—manned the beach post and coped with a variety of emergencies. One boy sliced his foot open with a broken bottle; another came to them complaining of stomach pains and they diagnosed the case correctly, summoned an ambulance and got the boy to hospital just in time for an appendicitis operation.

Few of their patients who came to the two young St John Ambulance men on the beach that summer can have realised that they were in fact approved school boys, serving out their time at Wellesley. Both Jim and Roy had discovered an occupation in which they were needed, and in which they had proved themselves capable: and therefore both of them were happy.

Jim's school report had said that he was, at 15, sly, difficult and lazy. His reports from Wellesley said that he was adaptable, cheerful and willing; his seamanship instructor wrote, 'I have yet to hear him grumble.'

As a result of this experience Jim changed his ambitions. He gave up the idea of going to sea. He was due to be released from Wellesley but applied to stay on for an extra two months so that he might take his final first-aid qualifications. That achieved, he found a place as a trainee male nurse in a hospital: and the last report on him was that he was still happy and successful there.

On paper, Jim is probably not an outstanding advertisement for the Award Scheme. He never even reached his Bronze standard in all the sections that would have entitled him to a certificate. Yet he would probably have passed the fitness tests, since he was a keen sportsman—in the school cricket XI, the athletics team and the cross-country team. A well-built healthy young man, he would not have found the expeditions tough.

And yet, though Jim will never get an Award Scheme certificate, he is a fine example of the spirit that motivates it—the introduction to young people of wider interests. The courts said that boredom was probably the main reason why, at 16, Jim broke into a shop. At Wellesley he found an interest that no longer bored him. Evidently—like a long-distance runner—he had enough individuality to need to express it. It wasn't the chance to conform, or the chance to 'go straight', but the chance to do something constructive and positive that appealed to him.

Wellesley, with other approved schools, has adopted the Award Scheme because it provides a way of opening windows on to wider experience for those who, like Jim, are blinkered by the narrowness of life in a big city, even if it is materially wealthy.

Of the 141 young men at Wellesley at any one time, all are taking some part of the Award Scheme. Each has a record card which is marked up when he has reached a first, second or third series standard in any of the four sections of the Scheme: and in the course of time dozens of boys have been awarded the Bronze or

Silver certificate. Not unnaturally, many of them appreciate that the stigma of having come from an approved school is much reduced, when they try later for jobs, if they can also say that they have gained a Silver Award, and can produce a book to prove it.

One of the most popular of the 'public services' is Civil Defence, which happens to be particularly strong in the north-east and concentrates on the rescue and civil-aid aspects of the service. Wellesley's connection with CD started when some of the boys were recruited to act as 'casualties' in a rescue exercise. They proved to be excellent actors: and soon they were invited to take courses of their own.

As Wellesley is on the bleak Northumberland sea coast and has so strong a historic link with the sea—from 1868 to 1914, under one name or another, the school was on board a square-rigged sailing-ship moored near the mouth of the river Tyne—the coastguard service also takes an interest in the school and runs a 'public service' course for the Award Scheme. Yet more courses are organised by the local Red Cross and (in life-saving) by the Blyth police. For some years Wellesley boys have been helping with the restoration of the old harbour at Seaton Sluice, and not long ago won a Guinness Pioneer Award for their labours there.

Hobbies at Wellesley range from aero-modelling through marquetry and photography to woodwork. But some of the greatest enthusiasm is reserved for the expeditions. As new entrants, the boys are taken on simple expeditions into the Cheviots. But for the Award Scheme expeditions they are volunteers, under the guidance of staff members who go out in pairs.

Unlike some closed communities that have extremely luxurious camping equipment, Wellesley gear is simple and basic and well worn and well weathered.

The expeditions are done in series: for the first, a group will probably consist of about eighteen boys, but then one or two will decide that they don't like it. They are allowed to drop out of the group, until by the time of the Bronze expedition there will usually be about ten boys in the group, who go out in two sections.

There are certain much desired rewards for those who go on the tough expeditions of winter. There is often a long camp in the summer in the Lake District, and another group will perhaps cross

Fire prevention is a service with an obvious use
in a big factory. A fire captain at Park Gate
instructs a team of Award candidates

David Rogers, one of many hundreds of qualified adults
who give time to act as voluntary instructors
in different aspects of the Scheme,
demonstrates the correct way to put on a bandage

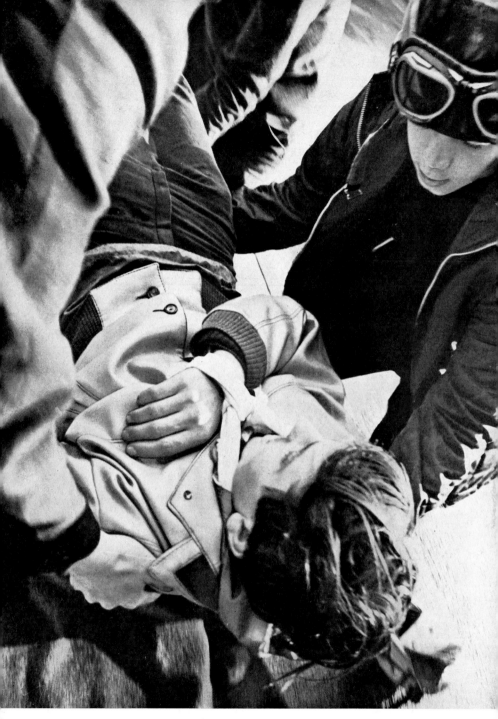

First aid has a practical value, as these boys learn
by treating a 'casualty' after a
mock motor-cycle accident

The art of camping is in making the most of limited resources. Surrey boys in camp on Dartmoor

Photo: Thomas A. Wilkie

Skill in many sports may count towards
an Award. Stephen Foster throws the discus

Physical fitness tests are done on the
works roads and verges. The individual time
for the distance is what matters,
not the competitive place. Here David Stables
(at Gold standard) and Roger Cox (at Silver)
stretch out for the 100 yards

George Cadman, a Gold Award holder and
assistant to the youth service organiser at Park Gate,
demonstrates the correct stance in archery,
a popular pursuit among boys

the Cheviots from north to south, doing some elementary rock-climbing on the way.

Other groups prefer canoeing: they build their canoes in the winter evenings, and then paddle them down rivers and canals in the summer.

Wellesley boys, some of whom have never before been out of their native cities (and they come from all corners of the British Isles to this sea school), become expert campers and climbers. So expert, in fact, that they are called on to act as umpires of others' expeditions. Recently in the Cheviots a group of youthful 'umpires' from the approved school trailed the members of an expedition round the hills, silently observing them from behind rocks and trees, and making their reports.

At the end of the day, in the bus on the way back to Blyth, the member of the Wellesley staff in charge of the venture found his boys looking at him oddly. 'Who were those people, sir?' asked one. 'Er—cadets,' said the master. 'They were coppers, sir,' said the boy. 'You could tell by their boots.' The master reflected that it was a fair piece of detective work.

In contrast to the story of Jim, consider that of Jean. This is very different, because Jean is thoroughly law-abiding and suffered from none of the frustrations that got Jim into trouble. Indeed, she had so much initiative that she virtually got herself through the Gold—an interesting and not untypical example of an individualist who did not much want to join a youth club but found that the Scheme gave her a means of exploring wider interests.

When she left school Jean breathed a sigh of relief. Not that she hadn't enjoyed Lady Mary's—she had. But now, at 16, she had a good job as an invoice typist in a Cardiff factory, a steady boy friend with whom she enjoyed going dancing, and the first taste of freedom. For some months she had a thoroughly good time. But her boy friend, then an apprentice toolmaker in an engineering works, was at night school several evenings a week: and on the nights when he was busy she would sit at home, feeling lonely.

She began to think about the busy times at school—not the schooling side of it, for she never much wanted to be academic. She missed the companionship, the sense of doing things. At school, for example, she had gone in for the Scheme and had reached the

D

Silver stage. For the Design for Living section she had first of all done a course on fashion (and had also designed, cut out and made a gingham dress); with her friends she had gone on an adventure walk to Cefn Or; as an 'interest' she had taken lessons in ballroom dancing, and had become very good at it; and she had done a course in first aid, and then another in child welfare. It had all been interesting and useful—and fun.

Sitting at home, she began to think that it might be amusing to try for the Gold. After all, she was within a short distance of it. But more than the gold badge, she thought that she would enjoy all the various activities.

One evening she talked it over with her father. He encouraged her to go on. There was only one snag: she didn't feel much like going back to school again. Nor did she much want to get tied up to any youth organisation that would try to run her life for her. Eventually Jean decided that at least she could find out what would be possible. She went to see the Deputy Head at Lady Mary's, who put her in touch with Miss Berenice Davis, who is Secretary of the Local Award Committee in Cardiff for the Girls' Award.

Miss Davis introduced her to the Heol Hir community centre, near her home at Llanishen, where there was a youth club with facilities for taking the Scheme. Jean didn't have to join the club— she was allowed to join the various courses that would enable her to qualify for the Gold. In the winter of 1963, for example, she attended a needlework class run by Mrs Andrews and made a princess-line dress—with a tight-fitting bodice and flared skirt. As another interest, she learnt to drive: her Record Book has an entry added by her boy friend, David, which reports (no doubt from experience) that she has a 'very good knowledge of car maintenance'.

For the Design for Living section she compiled a folder, illustrated with cuttings from magazines and catalogues, to show 'What to Wear and How to Wear It'. By this time she had changed her job and was working as a secretary in the office of the Clerk to the Justices in Cardiff: and when the time came for her to do a week's Adventure her employers generously allowed her to add the time to her holiday.

Not that the Adventure was much of a holiday for her. She went down to stay at a residential camp school run by the Cardiff

Education Authority by the sea at Porthcawl. There she was put in charge of one 'house' of girls from Cardiff schools, who go to the camp for periods during the summer. Though Jean enjoyed herself a great deal, organising play-readings, taking the girls swimming and running games on the sand-dunes, it was an extremely busy and demanding week. The time at Porthcawl went quickly and she came away with glowing reports.

As a further piece of public service, she spent five days working in the Suffolk House nursery, a Cardiff home for children under five who come from broken homes or are otherwise in need of care and protection. There she was able to put into practice the lessons she had learnt, some years earlier, while studying child welfare for the Silver Award. But here again she was doing work that she thoroughly enjoyed, bathing and changing the babies, playing with them, and taking the older children in twos to the park to see the swans. 'They really enjoyed it', she wrote in her diary-log of the week: and that enjoyment was much more important than the prospects of any badge.

Apart from these two special aspects of service, Jean had kept up her work with the Red Cross, and had become Assistant Commandant of the youth section of the Cardiff branch. She was also helping to run a pack of Wolf Cubs, where she is Rikki to the small boys.

When I met her she was wearing a beautiful dress of pale blue silk; she was lightly but elegantly made-up, and looked self-composed, very feminine and dazzling. Her fiancé, David, was with her, for they became engaged at the end of December 1964, in which month she finally qualified for the Gold.

David is rather older, and the Scheme had not been more than a pilot venture when he was at school and first going to work, so that in those days he had never heard of it and had not had the opportunity of entering for it himself. But he was most enthusiastic about Jean's part in it. In the eighteen months she had been working for the Gold their various interests—courses and social service for her, night school for him—had meant that they could only spend Wednesday evenings together: but they had been careful to reserve that one evening in each week to go out together.

Achieving the Gold Award—the badge was presented to Jean by the Lord Mayor at an Award ceremony in the City Hall—has

not meant that Jean has given up her various interests. She still keeps up her Red Cross work, and still helps to run the cub pack; and with her fiancé's encouragement she will go on with these things at least until they marry. Nowadays Jean never has to wonder what she can do to amuse herself: her life is very full from one week's end to the next. And also, if her humour and vivacity are any evidence, thoroughly satisfying.

4 The Scheme in the adult world

The Scheme is not confined to schools or youth clubs. Nor is there any reason why it should be limited to the youth service. If it has not been widely introduced outside this is mainly because adults who deal with young people in factories, shops and offices have not yet realised how they can help, and what pleasure they themselves can find in helping young people. But where the Scheme has been introduced into such places it has usually been a notable success. Take the example of Lewis's, the big department store in Glasgow.

Erica was an assistant working on the clock and watch counter when a notice came round to the younger members of the staff (there are usually 100 or 200 out of a total staff of 1,400) explaining the Scheme and inviting them to attend a meeting to discuss it. With her friend Beryl, Erica decided to go along and find out more. About eighty girls and thirty boys went to that first meeting; and half of them decided that they would have a go at the Scheme; and bought Record Books. Erica and Beryl found that they could go direct to the Silver.

For their hobby they investigated the history of Glasgow, discovering (to their surprise) that the city has some Roman remains. They visited the Hunterian Museum and the Art Gallery, and prepared a log-book of their findings, illustrated with maps, photographs and picture postcards. For their service section they were taken round by the WVS to help with the Meals on Wheels service, and visited a Glasgow Corporation children's home at Abbotsford Place—there they made friends with the children, most of them between 3 and 5, and took them to play in the parks. For the Design for Living section they attended lectures on the art of make-up.

Finally they went out on a series of Adventure walks organised by the store's Training Manager and Assistant Staff Manager, up beyond Loch Lomond in some of the beautiful country that is one of the great advantages of Glasgow life. Both Erica and Beryl qualified for the Silver, and twelve girls and six boys were presented with their badges and certificates in a ceremony at the store's restaurant, with the Senior Magistrate of Glasgow performing the presentation.

They decided to try for the Gold. For their service they went to help the orderlies at the newly opened Queen Mother Hospital: they soon realised how helpful they were being, for despite the newness and efficiency of the hospital, the staff were desperately overworked and the presence of the girls meant that the orderlies could sometimes be sure of ending their duty on time, instead of working for one or two hours over.

In the third week of August they completed their Gold Adventure. They were given a series of youth hostels to stay at—Loch Ard, Lendrick, Balquhidder and Crianlarich—and for six days had to walk in groups of four or five from one point to the next, planning their precise routes themselves from maps. On the third day it poured with rain, and they were glad to complete the twelve miles and get to shelter.

For the Design for Living section the girls were studying 'planning a home', particularly 'planning meals for the family'. Erica is a lively and amusing girl who says that the thing she has valued most about the Scheme is meeting so many people—people in the WVS, in the children's home, in hospital—whom she would not otherwise have known about. She says that her parents are very enthusiastic about the Scheme, but she has a boy friend, an engineer, who thinks that the whole business is a lot of time-wasting nonsense. Perhaps he won't think so if he ever becomes part of the receiving end of those 'planned meals for the family'.

The only qualification Erica now lacked was the period away from home: and this she would achieve by going on an Outward Bound course at Rhownair in Wales. Lewis's now book a number of places for their staff each year also at Carberry Tower, the Church of Scotland centre.

One of the young men doing the Gold while employed by Lewis's is Billy, who is just 18 and also a Scouter with the 8th Coatbridge troop, and hopes to get his Scoutmaster's warrant next year. For his public service Billy had been helping at Lauriston House, where he talks to and generally looks after people suffering from muscular dystrophy. He was taking his fitness tests at the Langside College of further education in Glasgow; unlike many Award candidates in Scotland who seem to choose pouring rain for the expeditions, Billy and his colleagues humped rucksacks over 3,000 ft peaks above Aberfoyle in blazing August sunshine.

By the end of 1965 Lewis's hoped to have twelve girls and six boys with Gold Awards on their staff, and another twelve girls and ten boys with Silver Awards. This will be a particular satisfaction to the General Manager, Mr V. Hanson, who started the

Scheme for his staff in the first place. He heard about it from his son, who came back from boarding school to announce that he was taking part in it. Mr Hanson realised from reading the literature about it that the Scheme could very well be a challenge, and an extra interest, for the young people on his staff. So he asked his Training Manager, Miss Ettie Irvine, to organise it.

Other adults on the store's staff voluntarily give help with the sort of special courses—on make-up, furnishing and home building needed for the Girls' Scheme. And the Assistant Staff Manager, Mr Allan Murray, helps to arrange the expeditions. Mr Murray joined the Glasgow store from Liverpool, and found himself enlisted in a Scheme already in progress (all this began at Lewis's three years ago).

He admits that when he arrived he knew very little about the Scheme and was not unduly keen to find himself landed with an out-of-hours activity: but now he is tremendously enthusiastic. 'You can't express the difference in the young people who do it,' he says. 'They gain so much confidence and assurance, and they enjoy it so much.'

Doing the Award Scheme requires some contribution from the store. The days that the young men and women spend out on expeditions, and in other Award activities, are deducted from their working hours and so the store willingly gives an appreciable amount of labour time each year. It has also provided three tents for the boys to take on their expeditions, though they and the girls must provide their own clothing and equipment.

The other contribution made by the store was the closing of the restaurant for an afternoon so that parents, friends and workmates of the Award winners might see them receive their badges and certificates from one of the city's chief officers.

To my mind, the working of the Scheme at Lewis's of Glasgow is an almost perfect example of the way it can be applied in industry and commerce, with great advantage to everyone taking part (the adults as much as the young people concerned) and a deal of pleasure in the participation as well. Lewis's do not use the Scheme as an extra inducement to young staff—one or two Award winners have subsequently left the store's employment, but have nevertheless been invited back to receive their badges.

.   .   .   .   .

The Scheme has also been introduced into other companies with a large number of young workers.

The Castle Works of Guest, Keen and Nettlefolds at Cardiff is one of the complex of steel works that stretches along the sea coast of Glamorgan. Like most similar factories, there is an apprentice training school in which young men joining the firm spend six months before going into the factory to learn their trade in detail on the shop floor. When boys, fresh from school, arrive at GKN they are given an introductory talk by the Education and Training Officer, Jack Morris. Apart from the local information about the company, its training methods and opportunities, Mr Morris shows each new entry the Duke of Edinburgh's Award film, *The Scheme*.

From that point it is entirely up to the boys themselves whether or not they volunteer to take part. If they do there are several company employees ready to help them, as instructors or assessors, and one who specialises in training the boys for their expedition into the Brecon Beacons. Most of them choose athletics for their pursuits, or judo or boxing. But not all. William was a member of the Barry and Vale of Glamorgan Archaeological Group, and produced with great pride a mapped and photographed log of the group's digs at Llandough during which they had found a couple of skeletons dating from the thirteenth century. This young man had been doing research in the Cardiff Central Library and Museum —not perhaps the most obvious pursuit for an employee in a steel works.

Brian and John were working on the Scheme because, they said, 'we saw the film and we decided to have a go'. Both had enjoyed the expedition in the Beacons, though it had been a long trek over rough country. For John it was no new experience—he had been out in the hills with the Boys' Brigade. But one new experience for them had been their turn of duty as helpers in a youth club for spastics, held in a Scout hall at Fairwater. 'We just talk to them and keep them amused,' said John. 'Guide them when they're playing table tennis, and that.' He talked as if it were the most ordinary thing in the world.

GKN at Cardiff has its share of Gold Award holders. Some break their connection with the Scheme as soon as they have achieved the Gold, and others continue as helpers for the younger people coming along to start the Silver. No one puts pressure on them to help, and so those who do it do so because of the satisfaction it gives them.

New industries have sprung up in South Wales, giving employment in the valleys long since hit by the depression in the mines— giving employment, also, to the wives and daughters of the valley families. On the site of the old Dowlais iron works, held in the curved arm of the Welsh hills, there is a group of factories one of which houses the Apparel Division of Kayser-Bondor. Here, amid the hum of a thousand sewing machines and the echoing pops of the BBC Light Programme, Mary (who is 17) works as a trainee supervisor, and Carol (who is 16) as a quality-control examiner.

The Girls' Award started in this factory when Miss M. J. Bishop joined the company two years ago as Assistant Personnel Officer. She had previously been Youth Officer for Red Cross and Guiding in Gloucestershire, where she was deeply involved in running the Girls' Scheme. But all her experience would have been useless had not the Kayser-Bondor management at Merthyr Tydfil allowed her to introduce the Scheme there as one of the services of the personnel department.

At present it is still very much a pilot scheme, with only a handful of girls participating. Mary joined because her elder sister joined. She had no great enthusiasm for it at the beginning, and just decided to do the Scheme 'for something to do'. However, it has already paid off. With a group of girls from the factory she took a course on electricity in the home (as the Design for Living section). This was run, in her own home, by the wife of a local bank manager, who took the girls through an elementary series of practical demonstrations of the right way to look after electrical appliances.

This showed them how to wire up a plug, how to mend a fuse and how to make sure that electrical appliances are safe. It has already proved its value for Mary. 'The plug of the telly at home came apart, so I mended it.' Her parents were very surprised. These girls are at the moment working towards their Silver Award, and as there is great enthusiasm for women's athletics in the valleys, they have been training every Saturday as an 'interest'. This also brought its reward when Mary won prizes for throwing the javelin, the long jump and the sprint at the factory sports. Mary, independently, may not even go on to take all the sections of the

Silver Award. She says, frankly, that she will 'see how things happen', which is honest. But for the moment she is getting a lot of fun out of doing the Award.

Carol is much quieter and more reflective. For her the highspot of the Scheme so far has been the Adventure walk which she did with two friends. They walked from Merthyr to Castell Coch, the mock-Gothic castle built outside Cardiff by Lord Bute, the great mine-owner, and now a classified 'ancient monument'. Before that Carol had never thought of going for any walk longer than the one down to the shops. For Design for Living she has been taking make-up and hair style; and for her 'interest' she is continuing the music she first started at school. She wants to continue with the Scheme. Now, as she says, she knows how to do various jobs in the house, which she didn't know before. Living in the midst of the hills, she has been introduced to them almost for the first time by the Scheme, and now says she will go out hiking again with her friends. But it is the usefulness of the other parts of the Scheme that appeals to her. 'After all,' she said, putting into a phrase the whole essence of the Scheme, 'it's just common sense, isn't it?'

If the Scheme is to be introduced into a factory or an office some adult has to take responsibility for it and also find sufficient qualified people to help, particularly with the pursuits and interests the candidates choose. But in a big organisation this is not insurmountably difficult. Most have clubs and societies for their members. Some are sporting, some have to do with the arts. So most organisations have the framework within which to run the Scheme for their younger staff, if someone would undertake to be in charge of it. Westminster Bank were lucky, since they had on their staff a man who had long been associated with youth work, and who had become Award liaison officer for Bedfordshire.

Avril is 18. She works in the Lothbury head office of the Westminster Bank on the administrative side of the staff department. Music has always been her hobby: she is a mezzo-soprano and sings in West London music festivals, and so music was an obvious choice for her Interest section of the Scheme. For the Design for Living section she was doing a course in flower arrangement, organised by the bank's horticultural society. And for Service she had, when I met her, spent three Saturdays working in a children's home. She was already fascinated by it: most of the children were illegitimate, some were coloured, and she was finding great joy in playing with them, telling them stories and generally looking after them.

Brenda lives at Highbury and Maureen at Clapham Common, at opposite ends of London: but they both work on the cheque-clearing machines at the Westminster Bank's Lombard Street office in the City of London. For their Design for Living section they have been attending courses on grooming and poise (of which they are fine advertisements). Both are keen on netball and were proposing to take a course on refereeing.

And on Tuesday evenings they were going to St Bartholomew's Hospital to classes in first aid. They had also done the first of their day adventures—a journey to Greenwich. Both were enjoying what they were doing perhaps more than they had thought they would when they started. At first they volunteered for the reason that they felt it was expected of them: but soon they found they were doing things such as the netball umpiring which would be immediately useful for the lunchtime games in which they take part.

They would also be taking lectures, in the Design for Living section, on house purchase, including such mysteries as how to get a mortgage, what snags to look for when starting a home and other aspects of home-making that they had never expected to know.

None of them found that the Scheme took up too much of their time. Perhaps fortunately, Brenda's boy friend was a holder of the Bronze Award and so knew all about the Scheme and was sympathetic to it. Their only difficulty was the amount of travel needed to get from place to place in London for the different sections they were studying in one week. For their athletics practice they had to travel down to the Bank's sports ground at Norbury in South London, which is convenient for anyone living on that side of the city, but a long evening's journey for anyone living to the north.

However, they had the satisfaction of knowing that as the Scheme has the approval of the bank's top management, they would be given extra time off to do their Adventure journey (though all other sections of the Scheme must be done in their own time).

These three were among the pioneers of the Scheme in a city

bank. Probably more city offices will join in due course, and it may then be possible to make corporate arrangements so that young people can take courses at lunchtime and as soon as they finish work. But these girls are proving that it is possible for the Scheme to be completed in the City under the conditions of today.

5 The handicapped

The scene was the ballroom at Buckingham Palace, all gilt, red velvet, mirrors and chandeliers. One by one the Gold Award winners at this winter presentation entered the great room in line, watched proudly by their parents and friends packed close together on the chairs and benches, while the Guards string band played, in the gallery, hit songs from musicals.

One by one the winners stood in front of the Duke of Edinburgh. The girls bobbed, the boys bowed: then they shook hands, paused to answer the Duke's questions about their uniforms, badges or crested ties, then took the proffered certificate, turned and walked away. For an hour and a half the Duke stood and shook several hundred hands, with precisely the same good humour at the end of the time as at the beginning. Girls in bucket hats, in pre-service uniforms, in school gym-slips, in rabbit fur, in silk; boys as police cadets, soldiers, sailors, airmen, schoolboys, close-cropped, Beatle-cut and with sideburns. Understandably, the Duke seemed to pick out the naval uniforms for particular conversations—except for one young soldier, his face glowing with the deep tan of some tropical station.

Then through the door, meticulously keeping his place in the queue, came a 17-year-old swinging his way along the carpet on arm-brace crutches. He pivoted round to face the Duke, and shook hands: and in the conversation that followed, the Duke congratulated John on being the first handicapped person to qualify for the Gold Award.

The Award Office issues a special instruction on the training and testing of the physically disabled. This states clearly that there is to be no lowering of standards.

'There are not two Award Schemes, one for the able-bodied, one for the physically disabled. The disabled have as good a chance of gaining Awards as the able-bodied, but not a better one. The one difference involved is in respect of physical activities in the curriculum of the Scheme, where a variation of target is permitted but not a reduction in effort or persistence. . . . The aim of each section in the Scheme must be achieved.'

None of this seems particularly applicable to John, because the most noticeable thing about him is his smile, which is cheerful,

direct and handicapped by nothing at all. Physically he is handicapped from the waist down, through early damage to his spine.
For five years he lived at the Shaftesbury School at Coney Hill
near Hayes in Kent. He is one of the oldest residents, for the school
only opened in its present form in 1959.

John's home is in Lincolnshire, at Woodhall Spa, where he went
on leaving school last year, hoping eventually to start his own
shoe-repairing business. His first move towards the Gold Award
at Coney Hill was—like many other boys—to become a Scout:
and not an inactive one. For his firefighter badge he took a test at
the West Wickham fire station, and passed. At this time the director
of the school, Mr Field, thought it would be a good idea if some of
his pupils might attempt the Award Scheme; so John was one of
the first to try.

The uninitiated might suppose that handicapped boys and girls
would have to be excused the expeditions: but they were not. Boys
and girls at Coney Hill are encouraged to go outside the school
and to learn their way about the ordinary world outside. In his
invalid chair John undertook a journey to Westerham, twenty-five
miles away, and back. His hobby was photography, and he did
better than merely take portraits of his friends or landscapes of the
surrounding country.

Film records are invaluable in a home for the handicapped, for
they vividly illustrate to both doctors and patients how the children
improve over a period of time. John became an unofficial medical
photographer, using the school's cine camera.

For both the Silver and the Gold standard John used his camera
for medical records and also for taking entertaining films of the
school's outings—to Chessington Zoo, London museums and the
local swimming baths, where the children are welcomed.

As the Public Service section of his Award he took a first-aid
examination at adult standard: and he virtually became an assistant
to the school's medical staff in looking after the smaller children.
It was said of him that his example in overcoming his own handicap
was the best guide that the younger children could have had, and
one that made tremendous impact on them. For his 'fitness' test
John took up archery, and as he is in no way handicapped above
the waist, his powerful shoulders made him a good, and soon a
skilled, archer.

When the time came for him to tackle his Gold expedition arrangements were made for him to attend a long weekend at a summer school organised by the National Association of Youth Clubs, whose officers acted as adjudicators. He drove there in the motorised chair that he had now been given—though he unfortunately failed his driving test at the first attempt, and so had to be followed during his run on the public roads by the school driver in another vehicle. Once at the camp, John looked after himself and slept under canvas for the three days—a much more challenging test for him than for the average Gold Award winner.

He became the first Gold Award winner at Coney Hill, and the first handicapped boy or girl to reach this standard. By the time he went to receive his Award, with his parents proudly watching, the Shaftesbury Society's home had achieved nine Bronze standards and three Silver; and John's record made his contemporaries and juniors even more eager to copy him. So there is no doubt that in the future there will be many more Award winners at Coney Hill.

6 The continuing effect

The Scheme is 'a challenge to the individual'. But it would be surprising if as a result more young people did not come forward to help with youth work and to take a responsible place in the community. Already there are some hundreds of Gold Award winners helping others in this way. One is a young man in Swindon who is an electrician by trade.

As a boy at Hillcroft Comprehensive School, Balham, Travis took the Bronze and then the Silver Award. He enjoyed himself doing them: aero-modelling was his first pursuit, for the Bronze. For the Silver he turned to stage electricity, partly because his brother was acting in the school plays, and though Travis didn't want to act he thought it would be fun to be involved. So he did the lighting for several school plays, and became so involved in the skills of electricity that he decided on leaving school to take an electrical apprenticeship.

Meanwhile his family had moved to Swindon, in Wiltshire. He began going to a Swindon youth club, and through Mrs Ansell, of the Association of Wiltshire Youth Clubs, he met David Garnett, the Award organiser for the county. People sprang out of the ground to help him attain his Gold standard.

He was doing a day-release course at Swindon Technical College, and his maths tutor was physical training instructor at the grammar school, on whose playing fields Travis did some of his training and his fitness tests in the evenings. His parents were still furnishing their house in Swindon, so Travis became a 'handyman' for his Gold 'pursuit', put in new window-frames and rewired and re-decorated the front room. He was introduced to a youth club in Bristol with whom he did a training expedition on Exmoor, pre-paring for it by Sunday-morning visits to the house of Victor Hill at nearby Purton.

For his public service qualification it was arranged that he would attend a firefighting course at the Swindon fire station. Fortunately at that time he was working in Birmingham, and so was able to travel to Swindon on Wednesday evenings in time to attend the course—because he had to be at the technical college on Thursdays. He did the Silver and Gold tests in one mammoth course; and somehow, until the very end of the course when nothing could be done about it, the Fire Service authorities managed to overlook the fact that he was not formally enrolled in the Auxiliary Fire

Service, and so was attending 'illegally'. Of course, he passed.

Then a Gold expedition was arranged for him by Dick Allcock, with a National Association of Youth Clubs group in North Wales. And so, with four days to go before his 19th birthday—which was then the upper ceiling limit for the Gold award—Travis qualified, and in the summer of 1964 went to Buckingham Palace to receive his certificate from the Duke.

His success was due largely to his own initiative—once he found that in Swindon there were, in fact, people willing to go out of their way to help him, put his plans into effect, and arrange tests for him. It is probably significant that he has not let the matter rest there. With two friends, Alan and Tony, he helped to run a youth club at Cavendish Square on a new housing estate on the outskirts of Swindon. For all of them it means giving up each Friday evening, and also denying themselves the more sophisticated and creative satisfactions of their own longer-established club, St Mark's.

It seems likely that, whether or not they get any thanks for it, these young men will go on providing for other young people the sort of help that they themselves received, and valued.

7 The people who help

The Scheme depends not only on the young people who take part but also on the adults who help. Many adults may contribute towards the achievement of one Award. There are the people who suggest the Scheme in the first place, those who run the necessary courses in the various subjects and sections and finally those who test the candidates' achievements and sign the Record Book. There is an old Award story of one candidate who got a Gold, and was given a party by her youth club to celebrate—and over thirty-six helpers turned up, each of whom had played some part.

At the Gold stage a candidate is responsible for finding his or her own helpers, and to that extent supervising progress. But it is too much to expect a boy or girl of 14 or 15 to plan interests that will be followed for a period of years. The Scheme therefore needs help from three groups of adults. First, those who organise, as teachers, youth leaders or training officers. Secondly, those who encourage, as parents or employers. And thirdly, those who act as tutors and assessors; who, being knowledgeable in many skills, some of them rare and unusual, give their time and trouble to keep up the tenacity of young people who are keen to learn but need the stimulus of expert advice and guidance.

The Scheme is very complex. Its provisions are set out in syllabuses published by the Award Office for both the Boys' and the Girls' Awards. There is a special booklet giving detailed advice on the preparation and running of expeditions; and there are two thick pamphlets listing the agreed syllabuses for the pursuits (for boys) and the Design for Living section, and interests (for girls).

In the latter each syllabus is preceded by a statement that it is for guidance only: 'The basic principle of assessment in this Section of the Award Scheme is the interest, progress and genuine sustained effort shown by the candidate during the stipulated minimum period . . . and not the attainment of any fixed standard.' The reason for this is well known. The Duke of Edinburgh believed, and most educationists agree, that it is a good thing to encourage young people to concentrate on one activity for a period of time, and that this promotes the 'stickability' that the Duke wanted to stimulate.

Because the Scheme was intended to encourage young people to find themselves by doing things that they enjoyed, the range of possible pursuits and projects was made as wide as possible—and the handbook is not exhaustive. The Award Office will always try to work out a syllabus for a particular interest if some youngster wants seriously to try it, if there is an adult helper available to give assistance with it, and if it is a creative and reasonable pursuit.

But one result of this great freedom has been that there have been different standards applied in different parts of the country, and even in different organisations within the same town or city, for the pursuits and interests. Of course, this section is only one-quarter of the requirements of the whole Scheme at any stage: the other three sections can be measured by more definite standards. And the alternative to this necessarily flexible system would be a rigorous series of examination-type standards: and that would certainly be less acceptable, both to young people and adults, than the present arrangement, with all its possible unfairness. It is also impossible to devise any workable system of measuring precise achievements in some of the pursuits.

The other aspect of the Scheme which has aroused some comments relates to the way it is run in schools and other closed communities, compared with its use in youth clubs and other open communities. Youth leaders sometimes argue that it is much 'easier' for young people in schools and pre-service units to get Awards, because they are under a fixed discipline already, while those who do the Scheme 'outside' are under no such control and cannot be guided in the same way.

There is a strict regulation in the Award Scheme that it must be voluntary. But it depends what you mean by voluntary. There are many schools in which the boys and girls of a certain class, usually at 14, 'volunteer' to take part in the activities that will lead to the Bronze Award. They are required by the rules to do these activities outside school time, but many schools adopt a generous attitude to the use of time for Award activities. In any case, there are some schools—such as the independent boarding schools—where boys' and girls' lives are regulated from getting up to going to bed, and there is virtually no free time at all in the sense that boys and girls living at home and going to day schools recognise it. In those schools the Award Scheme obviously has to be fitted into school programmes, if it is to be done at all.

The results of the Scheme in the last ten years show that a considerable number of boys and girls achieve the Bronze standard at school, and then when they leave they drop the Award Scheme as they drop everything else connected with school. This has been called the 'fall-off', and can be seen clearly in the statistics. So some people argue that the Scheme should be taken out of school altogether.

But there have been many instances when young people, having started the Scheme at school, have dropped it for a time and then come back to it on their own initiative later. If only a few hundred examples like that happen each year the efforts to get the Scheme going, particularly in modern and comprehensive schools, at the Bronze stage are certainly worth while. And there are many more examples. There is a school in North Wales where the girls, with little adult prompting, planned their projects and pursuits so that at the end of their course they could provide a concert and a party for the local old people's home. They did the catering, entertaining and all the other work. They also raised funds for the party. Afterwards they found they had £17 over. Some favoured buying the old people a transistor set, so that the bedridden could listen to the radio. But eventually they decided to keep the money in a fund so that each year they could send a small present and a card to each old man and woman in the home on his or her birthday, and thus maintain a link for months, if not years, with the old folk.

The amount of stimulus given by teachers is bound to vary with the character of the teacher concerned. Some teachers get whole classes genuinely to 'volunteer' for the Scheme by the warmth and force of their own personalities. There is no coercion here: but the personal influence of an imaginative teacher in the running of the Scheme can often be seen by implication in the cases where the Scheme suddenly fades out in a school when the teacher who ran it leaves to go elsewhere.

There is little to be done about this, except for more teachers to become aware of the Scheme and to be willing to make the very considerable effort required to run it, as a voluntary service. But the way the Scheme is run is bound to differ from organisation to organisation, since so much responsibility is given to the 'operating authority'. In a forces unit the Scheme is bound to take on a military flavour; in a youth club it will be much more free-and-easy. This is part of the Scheme's virtue: it can be adapted to many different uses in many different contexts. This was how it was planned, and this is how it works.

The Scheme can be done, and has been done, by individuals who belong to no youth organisation. Between 2,000 and 3,000 have achieved Awards in this way each year. They must, of course, join in with other young people for certain parts of the Scheme, such as the Expedition.

The 'fall-off' of young people who, leaving school, do not continue with the Scheme beyond the Bronze stage parallels the young people who, on leaving school, do not join youth clubs or any other organisations. The young are not organisation-minded.

'The society which adolescents now enter is in some respects unusually fluid . . .' was the description given by the Albemarle Report on the Youth Service in 1960.

'Old industries change their nature as new processes are adopted; new industries appear and help to shift the location of industry itself. New towns arise, and new estates on the outskirts of old towns deplete the established housing areas and alter their social composition. A series of Education Acts, notably that of 1944, are causing some movement across class and occupational boundaries and should in time cause more. So British society is beginning to acquire greater mobility and openness. The effects of these changes are not always marked at present; some groups seem to live much as they have lived for many years. Yet as the changes develop, so old habits, old customs, old sanctions, old freedoms and responsibilities will be called in question and new relationships demanded . . . These changes are *of* the new world of adolescents. They, trying to find their direction without so many customary signposts, perhaps without the long-established habits of a steady local life, will be put under special strains. For these changes, towards what we have called a greater openness and fluidity, leave the individual more exposed, demand a greater number of deliberate and individual decisions. Yet paradoxically this society is increasingly organised and set into formal patterns. Adolescence is always a period in which the energies and growing needs of individuals conflict with the customs, the necessarily restricting adult customs, of society as a whole. So much is unavoidable. Different societies have greater or less success in allowing adolescents to arrive at their own kind of maturity without damaging themselves or society in the process.'[1]

One of the notable successes of the Award Scheme has been in bridging the gap between youth and maturity, and between young people and adults. Young people have great freedom in the 1960s: economic freedom, social freedom. Whole industries, particularly in pop music and clothes, are devoted to attracting them, and the spending power of the teenage market is a substantial factor in Britain's economy.

The Award Scheme is most successful when it links the young with the adult world in a common aim, whether this is the care of the sick or the elderly or the following of a shared pursuit. This is why adult 'helpers' are so vital to the success of the Scheme, and why, if and where the Scheme becomes weak, it is because of the failure of the adult world to spare time for it.

There are now fifty-two Award Liaison Officers in England and Wales. They give their spare time to helping the Scheme in two ways. They are a source of information about the Scheme in their own districts, and can assist and encourage organisations in their part of the country who want to know how to introduce or work the Scheme. Secondly, they provide a means by which the Award Office can get information about the way the Scheme is going. These men and women often give a great deal of time and energy to helping the Scheme, though they are not paid for it. They may— and many do—attend meetings of local Award Committees or Youth Committees when asked to give advice, but they are not members of the Award Office staff. (There are now about 300 Local Award Committees in the cities and towns of Britain at County or County Borough level.) But simply because they are independent people they provide focal points all over the country and are now essential to the running of the Scheme. Without their help it would hardly be possible to keep the organisation going unless there were an Award Office in each town. From the beginning the policy has always been to let operating authorities use the Scheme and thus keep the costs of administration down to the minimum.

1. Report of the Committee on the Youth Service in England and Wales (the Albemarle Report), HMSO Cmnd 929, 1960.

But many of the Award Liaison Officers take a very practical part in the working of the Scheme. One of them skippered the British yawl *Tawau*, which in the summer of 1964 competed in the Tall Ships Race to Bermuda and was the second ship to cross the finishing line. Incidentally, there were seven Award holders in the crew, and the navigator was the secretary for the Boys' Award.

In recruiting adult help the girls are in a much more favourable position than the boys. This is because, in general, women band together for social purposes in a way that men do not. In many places the Girls' Awards have been given immense help by the WVS, Women's Institutes, Townswomen's Guilds, Soroptimists, Inner Wheel and so forth. In most towns there is no shortage of qualified women to teach and test the various aspects of the Girls' Awards, from make-up and hair styles to dress designing and floral decoration. If the WVS cannot find one of their own members to do the job there is usually a friend of a friend who proves willing to help.

This sometimes needs patience. 'A week spent fruitlessly seeking a co-operative bee-keeper for a girl who fancies this activity as her interest is bound to be crowned with the news that she has decided to do ice-skating instead.' Some towns have organised lavish help for the girls: in Oxford, for example, almost every street has a woman representative of the Girls' Awards ready to give information, advice and help.

The Award for boys has suffered all along because men do not act in this way. They get together in Rotary, the Round Table, the British Legion, Toc H and in Trades Councils and branches of trade unions. But with rare exceptions they do not have the time to give to the Scheme that their wives have. There are distinguished exceptions: the Rotary Club in Barry, South Wales, has produced an excellent printed guide to social service and youth work in the area; and the Luton Advisory Committee for the Award Scheme was started through the work of the Luton Junior Chamber of Commerce.

A fairly typical example of what happens in a small town is the experience of Guildford, Surrey. Guildford has its own borough youth service, which reckons to be in touch through its clubs (including church clubs) with about 3,000 of the town's 5,500 young people between the ages of 14 and 20. When the present

Many boys choose motor-cycle engineering
as their pursuit. Don Hancock demonstrates
with a cut-away engine

The boys' expedition can be, and often is,
done by canoe—frequently built by
the candidates themselves

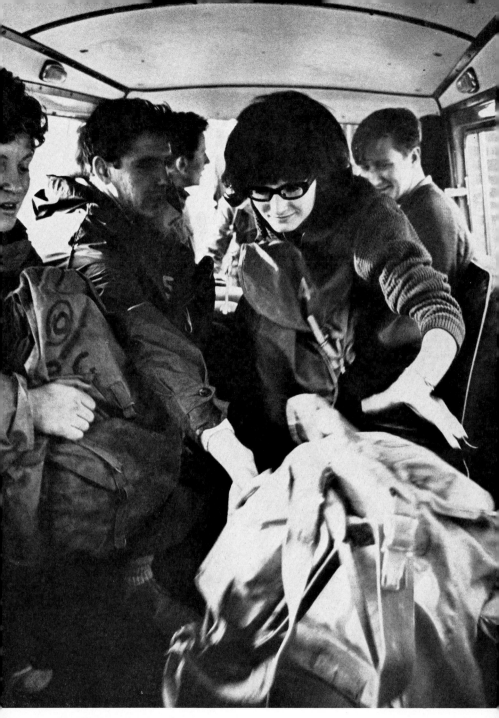

Anne Bath setting off with her friends
in the works minibus to begin her adventure trek
for the Gold Award

Drama is a pursuit that youth groups
particularly enjoy. Anne Bath, George Cadman
and Robert Hutchinson rehearse a play
for a festival

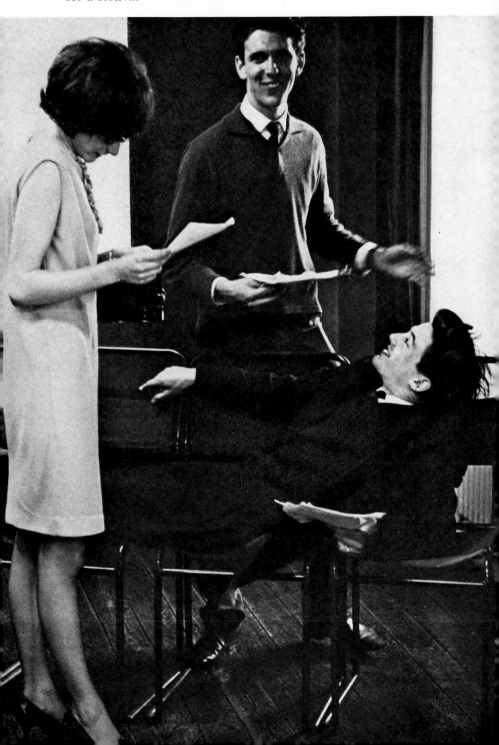

The girls' Design for Living groups
are instructed by adult experts
who visit the works for lunchtime sessions.
Janet Walker and Anne Sargeson engrossed
in the intricacies of floral decoration

'They had also gone the first of
their day adventures . . .' Brenda, Maureen
and Avril from the Westminster Bank
mapping a walk

The dancing may not be competition standard
but the works training centre
makes a good ballroom

'He discovered that he could use his interest
in stage lighting as his pursuit. . . .' Robert Page
at Woodberry Down

youth organiser, Mr Tait, came to Guildford from the West Country in 1960 the Award Scheme was being operated in the town independently by the Air Training Corps, the local Sea Cadet Unit and by some Red Cross nursing cadets. One of the Guildford schools, the Northmead Secondary, was also encouraging its boys to take the Scheme, and three of them had qualified for the Bronze.

The Guildford Youth Committee, prompted by its youth organiser, decided to launch the Scheme. From the beginning there was a good Press: each of the local papers runs a 'youth column'. The provincial Press has generally been favourable to the Scheme, and many entrants can be traced directly to the sight of a picture of a Gold Award winner in the local paper.

In February 1962 a public meeting was held in the Guildford Guildhall with the then Mayor as Chairman. Invitations were sent out to adult organisations and youth groups, and about ninety people attended. An Award Advisory Committee was formed. Two civic youth clubs had part-time paid leaders: they agreed to help. One 'old Gold', Andy Champness, became responsible for looking after candidates who were 'unattached', belonging to no social club or organisation but doing the Scheme on their own initiative.

As a first step the central committee set out to provide facilities that the individual groups might find difficult, if not impossible, to provide, such as co-ordinated training in first aid, Civil Defence Rescue and Fire Service. Bronze and Silver expeditions were to be done in the Surrey hills, and Gold expeditions either on Dartmoor or in North Wales. For the girls, a Design for Living course was organised in the Red Cross headquarters. In the first year, on a controlled and limited entry, eighty young people took part: forty-two Awards were presented by the Chief Constable of Surrey at the end of the year, together with three that had been gained earlier by boys at Northmead School.

The experience of this year showed that the weight of running the Scheme was falling on the youth organiser and the youth-club leaders. A special committee of Guildford people, chaired by Mr D. P. Herbert, a solicitor, prepared a report. This gave as a condition for further expansion that more adult helpers must be found. Seventy likely men and women were personally invited to a

F

meeting. Thirty-five turned up and agreed to help. At the end of the year about twenty were still helping. But nearly all of them were men and women whose work was normally with young people—teachers, club leaders and instructors in pre-service units. The remainder had become bored or were 'too busy'. The youth organiser had planned a system of helpers (rather like the street-by-street system organised among the women of Oxford, though he did not know of it): but he could not find the people.

There is a possible source now beginning to be tapped. Many of the boys and girls who have already achieved Gold Awards have come forward to offer their help. Not all can spare much time: many have full working lives, or are taking night-school courses, and more than a few have recently married and are naturally preoccupied with making a home. But it is likely that the Scheme will draw much support in the future from those who have done it and recognise its value.

Some places—Surrey is one—have associations of Gold Award winners. In each case these are locally organised, because the Trustees have decided that there shall be no official or central 'old boys' and old girls' ' club. This is because it is the policy of the Scheme not to regard any of the Awards as steps towards the creation of a social élite, an 'in-group' of people who think them-selves better than other people. The Scheme is an individual activity, not an exclusive club.

If the Scheme makes such demands on adults can it thrive? The answer, plainly, is yes, judging by the separate experiences of many operators. Most operators say that they never find any difficulty in persuading an adult 'expert' to help, and then to test, a young enthusiast with a pursuit or interest if the youngster is genuinely keen. Sir John Hunt tells of meeting an elderly pigeon-fancier in the north who was helping a candidate with his hobby, and both of them getting immeasurable enjoyment out of it.

But the difficulty here is that someone must search out the adult helpers. All too often, particularly at the Bronze stage, young people are persuaded to choose as their 'pursuit' or 'interest' a subject that is administratively convenient for the school or club to run courses in.

Few teachers or youth leaders have the spare time to go searching for adult helpers, and then spend perhaps hours explaining the

Scheme to them and persuading them to help. This may become easier as more people become aware of the Scheme, its purpose and its method. Some Local Award Committees have tried to compile lists of willing helpers in their district, only to find that when approached later these helpers prove either to be 'too busy' or else offended that they have not been approached before. Adults can get bored and irritated as easily as adolescents: and some have been put off by the sometimes casual attitude of the young people they go out of their way to help. The professional youth leader is used to this attitude: the layman is not. Yet the Award Scheme depends on the willing help of many more adults in all walks of life if it is to expand.

8 How the Scheme started

There has always been talk among adults about the faults and failings of young people. Ten years ago the talk was louder than usual. The country was becoming prosperous again, and young people who left school at 15 were soon earning considerably more money than their parents had done when they were the same age. There was more leisure time in which to spend the money: soon whole industries sprang up, particularly in pop records and clothes, to amuse and satisfy the young.

And yet many young people, finding no satisfaction in these things, became bored. Some, largely out of boredom and looking for kicks, got into trouble with the law. Others soon became disillusioned with the 'affluent society' their elders were so proud of, and passionately followed any cause that seemed to proffer a serious and idealistic purpose (the Campaign for Nuclear Disarmament was one).

There was much talk about what should be done, but the world of the adult and the world of the young were split apart. Perhaps it was that the inhabitants of both worlds were disillusioned in different ways: men who had fought in the war found, ten years after it ended, that their victory had come to seem hollow. They had fought for a better world, and found only a materially comfortable one, yet one with new threats in the headlines of each day's newspaper. A cult of romantic nostalgia began, producing books and films about the hero-figure fighting against odds.

Young people did not easily take to wearing uniforms when they could afford to buy themselves the latest fashion in clothes. Youth clubs, many without funds for adequate equipment, provided less attraction for young people who could buy their own record players and have parties at home, or who could easily afford the price of a nightly cup of coffee at a coffee-bar.

Schools faced the same disadvantage. With little money and no means of challenging the massive flood of propaganda aimed at attracting the buying-power of the young, some teachers understandably lost heart. Facing classes of forty and fifty in the primary and secondary modern schools, and classes of lively individuals who wanted only to get out and into the adult world, comparatively few had the energy or enthusiasm to run activities outside the classroom. Teachers started to take spare-time jobs to keep up the standard of living of their own families, and many schools became mechanical factories for teaching the bare elements of reading, writing and arithmetic between 9 am and 4 pm. In the grammar schools things were better, but not much better, as the battle to get into the universities hotted up. The young were out on their own.

Town boys and girls stayed in the towns, and young people in the rural districts flocked to the towns for work and amusement. Their lives were vigorous, entertaining and shallow: and when some created their own excitements, riding motor-bikes or scooters to seaside resorts, they were treated as anti-social hooligans and reacted in character.

On the other hand a minority, quite a sizable minority, did excellent and usually unchronicled work visiting and helping old people, carrying their coal, painting their rooms, reading to them. When the opportunity was made young people were eager to help.

But the narrowness of so many young lives depressed older people, who realised what enjoyment and satisfaction the young were missing and who wanted to open up the many existing opportunities for real enjoyment in Britain. The Duke of Edinburgh was one among many who saw this situation and wanted to remedy it.

Another 'youth organisation' was not the answer. Young people did not want to be 'organised'; they were thoroughly confident of their own abilities. During the Duke's own boyhood, at school in Scotland, he had taken part in an experiment. His headmaster, Kurt Hahn, had devised a scheme by which the boys of Gordonstoun, the high school at neighbouring Elgin, and the fisher boys of Lossiemouth would all be able to participate in a scheme under which they would attempt to reach certain standards. These standards would not be competitive; they would apply to fitness, to some form of public service, to hobbies or other interests. At the end of this scheme the individual who had proved his own capacity for sticking at his chosen interests would qualify for the 'Moray Badge'. During the war Dr Hahn had tried to persuade local authorities to participate in a comparable scheme for young people all over Britain, to be called the 'County Badge', but wartime demands on people's time were too pressing.

The Duke valued the breadth of his own education—the out-of-school training as much as the academic. He spoke about it once, appropriately in Scotland in 1949: and his words give a clue to the motives that were later to impel him to start the Award Scheme:

'My earliest instruction in the art of seamanship', he said then, 'was received at the hands of a Scottish trawler skipper, and in the process I discovered the east and west coasts, as well as that unique piece of water, the Pentland Firth. All this stood me in good stead during the years of the war.

More recently I have had the opportunity of wandering over the hills and also of doing some fishing. These pursuits, with the moments of solitude and reflection which they give, are invaluable to any man who is trying to keep a balanced outlook in the midst of the furious activity of modern life . . .'

The Duke went on to speak of the wartime kindness of the people of Edinburgh to visiting sailors like himself, and continued:

'There are in this world hundreds of things which are *right* but which cannot be legislated for—things which will never be done unless someone is prepared to do them for no reward except possibly a clear conscience.

Once upon a time it was a relatively easy matter to clear one's conscience by contributing money to various charities and organisations which set out to do the *right* thing. This method is not so easy now and yet there is just as much to do. It will be fatal for us if we ever come to think that merely by passing laws we can get out of our responsibilities towards our fellow men.'

The idea of a nation-wide scheme of awards for young people stayed with the Duke. He called together a committee for interested people and together they drafted a scheme, which was discussed in 1955 with the Minister of Education. He suggested that such a scheme might be administered within the framework of the existing national voluntary youth organisations. In the early stages the King George's Jubilee Trust had provided an office and (in the person of its secretary, Major-General T. N. F. Wilson) an adminis-trator.

In 1956 national service was still operating in Britain. Young men were 'called up' at 17½ or 18 to serve for two years in the forces. When the Scheme was started, therefore, it was seen by many as a bridge across the time when most boys left school at 15, and the time when they went into the services.

Some of the youth organisations that were approached were enthusiastic. Others, including at first some in the Boy Scout movement and other organisations with badges and tests, were not so enthusiastic: they were immersed at the time in the preparation for a world jamboree and in any case felt that they needed no experiment in youth service. Later, it is fair to say here, they came to appreciate the full value of the Scheme, particularly in the years when many young men give up practical Scouting: and now there is an arrangement that Queen's Scouts are considered to be at the Silver stage of the Award Scheme, and may continue directly to work for the Gold.

The King George VI Foundation, created to spend the money contributed as a memorial to King George VI in the service of the young and the old, gave a grant to enable the Scheme to start. Sir John Hunt, who had been a member of the originating committee, was appointed secretary, a title later changed to Director, and in February 1956 the Duke of Edinburgh's Award Scheme was announced to the public.

After an important conference at Ashridge in April 1956 three changes were made in the planning. First the age limit was lowered to 14, so that boys at secondary modern schools could start the Scheme before they left at 15. This was to try to interest the many boys who, on leaving school, preferred independence to membership of any club, pre-service unit or other youth organisation— the 'unattached', as the statistics called them. The second change was that some local education authorities asked if they might introduce the Scheme into their schools. Originally the Scheme was intended to be outside school life, but this request from the local authorities was granted on condition that the Scheme was not made part of the school curriculum. Thirdly, the services and some independent schools and direct-grant grammar schools asked if they might join in.

It is important to notice that, although schools are among the keenest users of the Scheme, it was not at first intended for boys and girls at school, but rather for those who had recently left.

With the ending of national service in 1958 the Scheme became 'open-ended', and entirely new problems started, problems that were to lead eventually to the raising of the upper age limit for qualifying for the Gold.

By the end of 1959 it was estimated that 30,500 boys and girls had started to work on the Scheme. There were over 200 operating authorities: about half are now Local Education Authorities. Obviously the Scheme was going to be a success: and so in 1960 the Scheme ended its pilot or experimental phase and became the Award Scheme proper. By this time, also, it had given birth to its own magazine, *Gauntlet*, which was edited and published by the Award Office in Wales.

At the beginning everyone agreed that the Girls' Awards should be different from the Boys'. A drafting committee under the chairmanship of Dr McAllister-Brew prepared the syllabus that was the basis of the present one for girls, with its special emphasis on home-making in the section called Design for Living—a title thought up by Mrs Margaret Forsythe, one of the drafting committee, after a visit to the Design Centre in the Haymarket. So in 1958 the pilot Girls' Awards were launched, with Mrs Gordon-Spencer as its Secretary. From the first, the many national organisations for women gave the Scheme great practical help.

In 1960 the Duke of Edinburgh attended a conference for members of Local Award Committees, called to discuss ways in which the Scheme should develop. (This was the first of a series of biennial conferences.) Throughout this early period no one was entirely sure how things would happen; and though there seemed to be evidence that young people valued the Scheme and enjoyed taking part, it was not yet possible to see to what extent the Scheme could work, and whether or not it would prove to be applicable to boys and girls in many different contexts. But two developments took place that were to have a considerable influence on the future: the Scheme was given a formal constitution, and the Ministry of Education (with, in Scotland, the Department of Education) gave the Scheme a grant equivalent (at that time) to half its expenses.

Local Award liaison officers, appointed as a means of monitoring the Scheme's growth, were men and women living and working in different areas who voluntarily agreed to act as 'focal points' for the Scheme, bringing together the local operating authorities, trying to arrange common provisions for courses and smoothing out differences.

The appointment of local liaison officers was a further move in the decentralisation of the Scheme. There was, of course, a danger that these authorities would interpret the conditions of the Awards with very great variation. This did happen: some boys and girls had to work hard for their Awards in some places, while in other places Awards were given much more generously. It was at this stage that the argument began to emerge that has recurred throughout these ten years. Some operating authorities argued that because the Scheme is first and foremost a test of (in the Duke's word) 'stickability', technical standards might be relaxed for pursuits and expeditions where a candidate was known to have tried immensely hard, but had not quite reached the standard set down in the Leaders' Handbook. Others—whose point of view seems eventually to have prevailed—argued that there is no sense in fixing standards if they are then to be ignored.

The formal constitution of the Scheme was set up in 1960 under the terms of a Trust Deed. Trustees[1] were appointed to support the Duke of Edinburgh, and these Trustees appointed fourteen members of an Advisory Committee, to which a further fifteen representatives would be nominated by a General Council of representatives from the operating authorities. The first meeting of the General Council—whose official duty is to be a consultative body for the working of the Scheme, and to advise the Trustees— was held under the Duke's chairmanship at St James's Palace on 20 December 1960.

At this stage the general pattern of the Scheme was becoming established. A great many boys and girls were going in for the Bronze at school (42,300 of them entered the Scheme in 1960). But about half of them dropped out as soon as they left school: possibly 30 in 100 continued to the Silver. It seemed that the Scheme might become associated only with schools and with schooldays, which was exactly what had not been intended in the first plans. Several moves were made in 1961 to persuade industry that the Scheme could operate successfully in factory and office training schemes. The Industrial Welfare Society organised conferences, and

1. At present (1966) these Trustees are: H.R.H. The Duke of Edinburgh, Robert Beloe, Miss P. C. Colson, Lt-Col V. A. J. Heald, Sir John Hunt, N. C. Macdiarmid, Alex Abel Smith and Lord Tangley. Robert Beloe is chairman of an Advisory Committee with thirty members, fourteen of whom are nominated by the Trustees and sixteen by the General Council.

the Trades Union Congress sent round a circular to Trade Councils recommending the Scheme to their members. A particular effort was made during Commonwealth Technical Training Week.

As an increasing number of boys and girls were training for Gold Award expeditions some method of co-ordinating and assessing these expeditions became necessary, and four Expedition Panels were set up (by people using the Scheme, not by the Award Office) for North Wales, Dartmoor, North Yorkshire and the Isle of Man. To help young people who might find it a financial hardship to do a Gold expedition training course, Sir Billy Butlin put a certain number of places at his camps at the disposal of the Award Office in camps near suitable training areas.

By 1962 all but eighteen of the 194 Local Education Authorities in Britain were licensed as operating authorities of either the Boys' or Girls' Scheme, or both. Some of the schools run by these author-ities were for handicapped children: and when it was found that some of these handicapped boys and girls were successfully com-pleting most sections of the Scheme, and were only deterred from achieving Awards by the impossibility of their reaching the required standards of fitness, variations were made to the Scheme. These in no way lowered the standards, but extended them to give a variety of alternatives to be used in special cases, so that a deaf, blind or otherwise handicapped boy or girl might still, with much the same quality of effort as that needed by someone with all his faculties, achieve an Award.

The numbers of entrants continued to increase. The peak year was 1963, when 43,300 boys and 19,600 girls entered the Scheme. In 1964 the numbers of entrants dropped slightly—to 41,360 boys and 18,400 girls. The figures are never complete, and it is not easy to be sure of the accuracy of them. The Award Offices only keep detailed records of Gold Award holders, and local operating authorities are charged with the responsibility for giving out and recording Bronze and Silver Awards, merely reporting the number of these to the Award Office once a year. A better and more accurate guide may be the number of operating authorities, which increased from sixty-two in the first year of the pilot Boys' Award (1957) to 512 in 1964.

That year also saw a doubling of the number of industrial companies, including shops, offices and other commercial concerns, taking part in the Scheme. Throughout the ten years of development all those concerned with the new Scheme had realised that the weak point of most youth activities was that so many young people started them at school only to drop them, with all other school activities, as soon as they left at 15. The appointment in 1964 of a member of the staff to be responsible for liaison with industry (D. S. E. Hayward) reflected this expansion, and his word encouraged it. In 1964-5 alone eleven companies were licensed to operate the Scheme, bringing the total to eighty-one: forty-five more are known to be using it through the agency of Local Education Authorities. A number of senior industrialists have been appointed Special Representatives for Industry, to encourage the use of the Scheme.

As the Scheme expands, it places still heavier burdens on the Award Office. The Office provides a service: it is not a youth organisation in its own right. It can authorise the use of the Scheme by other organisations. It can explain how the Scheme works and interpret the rules and conditions which—so that the greatest number of young people can take part—are necessarily complicated. The Award Office organises conferences and training courses for youth leaders, and generally acts as a practical link between the Duke of Edinburgh with the other Trustees and the various operating authorities.

In this way the Award Office is in touch with the 600 operating authorities and 253 Local Award Committees excluding those in Scotland, as well as with the Department of Education and Science, the Home Office and the service ministries. It keeps contact by sending its staff on personal tours of the country, and it is also responsible for organising the frequent visits that the Duke of Edinburgh himself makes to organisations running the Scheme. The Award Office charges no fees to the operating authorities for this service, and its income depends to a considerable extent on voluntary contributions from charitable trusts and commercial houses, and from promotions such as those organised by the Variety Club of Great Britain.

Though the essence of the Scheme is that it shall be run by the operating authorities throughout the country, and not by any central authority, the Award Office (with its subsidiary offices in Edinburgh, Cardiff and Belfast) is exceptionally small for such a busy point of reference. The London office consists of a narrow building in Westminster, staffed by fewer than a dozen executives (whose salaries are calculated in proportion to the Burnham Scale for teachers). Some are part-time. There is a small and overworked secretarial staff who somehow manage to keep cheerful while tripping over piles of parcels—publicity literature, handbooks, guides to the Boys' and Girls' Awards, and copies of *Gauntlet* (which is edited in Cardiff). To the enquiring visitor it is astonishing what a quantity of work and influence stems from such small space.

The London office houses Sir John Hunt, the Scheme's Director; Mrs Gordon-Spencer, Assistant Director and Secretary for the Girls' Awards; Commander David Cobb, Assistant Director and Secretary for the Boys' Awards; and F. A. Evans, the General Secretary. Attached to the London office are the part-time Secretary for Overseas Organisation; Major N. A. Johnson, the Special Representative for Fund Raising; and Mr Maurice Buckmaster, part-time Director of Public Relations. The Northern office in Edinburgh is run by the Scheme's Deputy Director, Mr W. T. Roe, who is also Secretary for the North; the Welsh office in Cardiff by the Secretary for Wales, Mr E. H. Prater; and the Belfast office by the Secretary for Northern Ireland, Mr R. Hicks.

No one regards the pattern of the Scheme as fixed for all time. In a period of rapid change the Scheme must change to reflect the changes in the world of the young. So in 1964, as the result of many discussions, the requirements for the Gold Award were changed. Certain things were added, such as the requirement that a young man or woman must spend a period of time away from home, living among other people in a context strange to them. And to fit the Scheme better into the lives of the young people doing it the age limit for boys was raised to 20 (as it had always been for the girls) to allow time for these extra efforts.

But all the developments of the Scheme are limited by the amount of money available. In the early days the Scheme was launched through the generosity of King George's Jubilee Trust and the King George VI Foundation. Since then it has been given many grants by these and other charitable trusts and foundations whose constitutions allow them to support youth work. In recent years the Ministry of Education (now the Department of Education and

Science) has given the Scheme an annual grant which in 1965 amounted to £13,500. However, the greater part of the Scheme's finances (£53,000 in 1953) comes from donations from private individuals, associations, organisations and firms. The Variety Club of Great Britain and the Grand Order of Water Rats have raised large sums for the Scheme.

The Scheme also has a Special Projects Fund, set up from the royalties of the film *Some People*, made in 1961 with Kenneth More as its star. The profits from this film were given to the Duke of Edinburgh by Nat Cohen, the Anglo Amalgamated Film Distributers Ltd., the Associated British Pictures Corporation and James Archibald, and the resulting fund has been used to finance the making of films including *The Scheme*, a colour film aimed at interesting young people, and *Debate*, a black-and-white film intended for adults.

How does the Award Scheme spend its money? The offices are small and modest, usually overcrowded with literature and files. So a great deal of money goes on travelling round the country, running conferences and meetings and paying the expenses of the Award liaison officers who give their time and energy to interest young people in the Scheme and to co-ordinate the vastly differing efforts of the operating authorities. The cost of all this is about £1 per head for each youngster entering the Scheme (£65,840 in 1963): but this represents an investment in the future, both because some of these entrants will become the operating authorities of the Scheme in the future, and because much of the day-to-day effort of the staff is directed towards persuading more young people to take part.

And, as a result, by the publication date of this book more than 450,000 boys and girls will have taken up the Duke of Edinburgh's challenge in the nine years that the Scheme has been operating. When one remembers that for the first three years the Scheme was a pilot venture of limited scope, and practically unadvertised, this is a remarkable achievement.

9 The Scheme overseas

One measure of the success of the Scheme is the interest it has aroused overseas, both from those who want to belong to it and those who want to start Schemes of their own along the same lines. From the first years of the Scheme there have been many enquiries of this sort. At first, individual groups were specially licensed as branches of the United Kingdom Office, provided they were within the Commonwealth. Not all were: individuals and youth organisations in Denmark, Germany, Holland, Israel, Korea, Mali, Norway, South Africa and Sweden have been interested in the Scheme, and following Prince Philip's tour of South America there were enquiries from Argentina, and Peru, as well as the United States of America, where the late President Kennedy's advisers asked for details.

It was clear that some policy would have to be worked out for the use of the Scheme overseas, partly to safeguard the standards of the various Awards. From the beginning it was laid down that as the Scheme carries the Duke of Edinburgh's name it would only be appropriate under that name within the Commonwealth. The Award Office gladly gives full particulars of the Scheme to visitors from other countries, and is pleased when those countries start up equivalent schemes under some other name. A successful example of this is the Scheme in Israel run on similar lines to the Award Scheme, partly initiated by the 'Bridge'.

By 1961 the Scheme was being operated overseas by some specially licensed authorities, by some voluntary youth organisations with overseas branches but headquarters in Britain, and also in Aden, Hong Kong, Sarawak, Jamaica, Kenya, Southern Rhodesia, Australia, Nigeria, Canada and New Zealand.

In 1962 Major-General W. A. Dimoline, formerly Colonel Commandant of the King's African Rifles, was appointed Secretary for Overseas Organisation. As General Secretary of the Inter-Parliamentary Union, which maintains relations with overseas parliaments and welcomes parliamentary groups from overseas to Britain, General Dimoline gave expert guidance to the introduction and working of the Scheme overseas until his death in 1965. At the same time Sir Percy Wyn-Harris, formerly Governor of Gambia, began a tour on behalf of the Award Office that was to lead to a new constitution for the Scheme overseas.

Following Sir Percy's tour, 'parallel' Schemes were started in Australia' Canada and New Zealand. Each of these countries now has a national council for the Duke of Edinburgh's Award Scheme, chaired in each case by the Governor-General, and responsible to the Trustees in London of whom the Duke is chairman. For the day-to-day running of the Scheme, three National Co-ordinators were appointed, as the Duke of Edinburgh's personal representative for Award Scheme matters, authorised to take decisions on his behalf relating to the day-to-day running of the Scheme. These are in Australia, His Honour Judge Adrian Curlewis; in Canada, Lt-Col Trumbull Warren, President of RHEEM (Canada) Ltd; and in New Zealand, Mr Philip Proctor, Managing Director until 1965 of Dunlop New Zealand Ltd. Each country also has an Award Office, which issues guides and handbooks to the Scheme.

The Scheme was launched in Canada in 1962, and although the Canadians found, as all users of the Scheme have done, that the shortage of voluntary adult helpers limited activities, forty-eight Bronze and nine Silver Awards had been gained in the first eighteen months.

In New Zealand the first meeting of the national council was held in July 1963, but it was able to take on a number of flourishing 'licensed users', and so the proportion of both entrants and Award-winners was high. Over a thousand young New Zealanders started on the Scheme in 1964, a year in which 140 boys and fifty-seven girls achieved Awards, including eight boys with Golds.

In Australia the number of entrants to the Scheme was smaller, but the number of Awards gained was greater in proportion: 120 boys and sixty-six girls.

Branch Schemes—directly responsible to London—are now operating in Aden, Barbados, Fiji, Grenada, Hong Kong, Jamaica, Kenya, Malta, Nigeria, Sarawak, Trinidad and Tobago and Rhodesia. The Schemes in Kenya and Nigeria may become 'independent' Schemes. There are several precedents for this; there is an organisation in Pakistan, the 'President's Scheme', and there is discussion about a similar one in India. In Malaysia it is hoped that an 'independent' Scheme to be called the Yang di Pertuan Agong's Award may shortly be expanded to serve the whole country.

The scheme in Nigeria has an interesting history. Its head-quarters is in the Citizenship and Leadership Training Centre, started by a group of British education and colonial officers at

Man O'War Bay in the Cameroons, and now (since the breaking away of the Cameroons from Nigeria) in the Northern Province, on the plateau above the mining town of Jos. 'Man O'War Bay', as the Centre is still familiarily called throughout Nigeria, provides training courses for young Nigerians rather on the pattern of Outward Bound in Britain. Although it still has a British Principal, Raymond Snowsell, the Centre, which is being kept up by the Nigerian Federal Government, will in a few years have a Nigerian staff. Since 1958 temporary instructors have been provided at Man O'War Bay by Voluntary Service Overseas, and the majority of these instructors, usually two a year, have been holders of the Gold Award. Several of them have helped to introduce the Scheme to the secondary schools of Nigeria, where a number of boys qualified in 1962 for the Bronze. It seems probable that the scheme will be continued in the future, probably as the 'President's Scheme'.

Overseas also the Scheme is being used by many of the schools set up for the children of Service families: a few local schools have also become 'licensed operators', the latest two in the British Solomon Islands and in Barbados (since incorporated in Branch Schemes and in India).

The development of the Scheme in the Commonwealth is clearly a matter of association. The 'Parallel' Schemes, in Canada, New Zealand and Australia, are likely to thrive by the same sort of natural process of success that has driven the Scheme forward in Britain. They have been started in much the same way, with a minimum of publicity and a great deal of hard work in organisation behind the scenes. There, too, the challenge to adults will probably be the key to the Scheme's expansion.

Elsewhere, and particularly in Africa and the Indian continent, the Scheme will no doubt be different from that in Britain for two reasons. First, the fact that the Scheme in Britain is inevitably linked with the person of the Duke of Edinburgh. Secondly, the countries of Africa and India do not yet have a social climate in which social service has much attraction for the young. The social pressures on the young are often to get an education as the path to a white-collar job in the city, a car and the power to order other people about. In Nigeria the Citizenship and Leadership Training Centre fights a noble battle of education in social responsibility,

and it is to the great credit of the Nigerians that they have con-
tracted to continue with it. This is still a small stone barely rippling
a large lake. Yet there is obviously a place for such a Scheme in
Africa and India, whose need for local leadership in agriculture,
medicine and social welfare is so vast.

10 Overseas expeditions

Sometimes the achievement of a Gold Award leads to greater adventure. Some Award winners are now asked if they would be willing to volunteer for Voluntary Service Overseas, which sends young men and women to the developing countries to work for a year as teachers, in social service schemes or (if they have the required skills) as medical assistants, engineers, electricians or nurses. Already a number of Golds have served for a year in this way before returning to their old jobs, or to the universities and technical colleges, in Britain.

There is sometimes a chance for another sort of adventure. This reflects the high standards of expedition training done for the Gold Award: for a number of young men have, after winning their Awards, been selected for expeditions overseas, some led by Sir John Hunt himself. First envisaged as a means of training youth leaders, the initial expedition took twenty-one Gold Award boys, with three youth leaders and fourteen experienced mountaineers and scientists, to Scoresby Land on the north-east coast of Greenland, in July and August 1960. Though several peaks had been scaled in the fifties, most of the region was still unexplored and the party was able to cross the peaks and also conduct geological and ornothological surveys. That expedition was organised by the National Association of Mixed Clubs and Girls' Clubs: all the Gold Award holders were at work, and were released by their employers to take part. In the same year an expedition sponsored by the YMCA, including twelve Gold Award winners, made a glaciological survey of the Svartisem Ice Cap in Arctic Norway.

In 1962 the girls enjoyed an expedition of their own, if a less mountainous one, when as a result of an invitation from the 'Bridge in Israel' and the 'Bridge in Britain' seventeen girls, led by Mrs Gordon-Spencer, spent a month in Israel. While on the trip, Mrs Gordon-Spencer was asked to advise on the establishment of a comparable Scheme in Israel. The girls toured the whole country, youth hostelling in the north and—after a thirteen-hour journey across the desert—a week's work in a kibbutz.

A still more complex and delicate expedition was organised in April 1963. A group of forty-eight people, among them forty-two young men from industrial firms or the junior services all holding the Gold Award or having completed the two-year course of the National Association of Youth Clubs, walked and climbed across

the Pindus mountains of Greece. This was an Anglo-Hellenic
Expedition and included, besides the British party led by Sir John
Hunt, members of the Hellenic Alpine Club and the Greek Army,
and some students from the Anavryta School in Athens.

The expedition was organised into three groups, each of mixed
Greek and British nationality, and mixed ages and experience.

Despite bad weather, with heavy snow, the journey of 250 miles
was completed successfully, and the members of the expedition made
many friends among the isolated villagers. With a few days remain-
ing at the end of the journey, one group carried out a work project
in a mountain village, carting tons of rock and sand and building
a bridge. A quantity of scientific data was also gathered. The only
black spot on this experimental but highly successful international
expedition was a car accident on the return journey, in which some
of the British party were involved and from which one member
died.

In December 1964 the Secretary of the Award Scheme, F. A.
Evans, recruited four Gold Award holders to accompany him on a
geographical and archaeological survey in Gambia.

As a result of the success of these expeditions in which Gold
Award winners played a notable part, plans were made for several
similar expeditions, among them a further international expedition
in the Tatra Mountains of Poland, with the co-operation and
participation of the Polish Mountaineering Club, and with some
Gold Award girls also in the party.

11 The future of the Scheme

'Oh yes, the Duke of Edinburgh's Award,' said one 16-year-old to me. 'They tried to get me to do that in the Air Cadets. They put me up a tree on the end of a rope, and the rope broke. I'm not doing *that* again.'

Any scheme that tries to satisfy all the people all the time finishes by pleasing nobody. The difficulty in constructing a framework such as the Award Scheme is to make it flexible enough to be useful to the greatest number of young people and yet keep certain desirable standards in mind. The danger, of course, is that the vehicle becomes so flexible that it is purposeless. People think of the Award Scheme in many different ways, partly because adults tend to think in compartments of class or status. 'Public schoolboy' is still a sure-fire identity for a newspaper headline: and in the same way adults tend to believe that they can visualise a person from the phrase 'grammar school boy', or 'secondary modern boy', or 'mod'. Most are now being replaced by the ubiquitous 'teenager': and few people under 25 use these classifications at all. So an idea that can be shared by *all* young people, as the Scheme can, is not strange to the young for whom it is intended, as it may be to many adults.

'The trouble with the Award Scheme,' said one headmistress to me, 'is that it's too unsophisticated. Young people are much more mature today.' She was wrong. The Scheme is sophisticated. But it has to be guided by adults, and it is they who may apply an unsophisticated flavour to it.

This problem of adult attitudes is vital to the continued success of the Scheme, at least until enough young people trained in it have come forward to take a greater share in running it.

But the Scheme does not specify that boys or girls should dress in a certain way before they take part—except for the expedition, for which safe protective clothing has to be worn. Nor does the Scheme specify religious observance, though the guides make this point:

'By going in for these activities, young people will be acquiring self-reliance; it is hoped that they will also be learning the satisfaction and the value of using their talents in the service of others. Both these qualities are important attributes of citizenship. But these alone are not enough; a spiritual faith is also needed. It is

neither desirable nor possible to test spiritual strength in connection with this Scheme, but it is hoped that leaders and all who
are helping will regard this aspect of a young person's progress as
paramount; for on this factor, interpreted in its widest sense, the
value of the Scheme will ultimately depend.'

This approach has been approved by the leaders of all the
churches. It places spiritual matters where they belong, in the
conscience of the individual, though it encourages leaders to discuss
religion. But it does not debar the youthful agnostic or atheist from
taking part.

When the Scheme was launched it is clear that it was partly
hoped to capture the imagination of those boys and girls who left
school at 15 and afterwards took no part in community life—who
were out on their own, ganging together for immediate amusement.
But this was not the only group for whom the Scheme was intended:
and it has not been limited to them.

But it can now be seen to divide, in practice, into two age-groups.
There are the 14- and 15-year-olds, doing the Bronze, usually in
groups by school class or age, and usually stimulated if not posi-
tively directed by some enthusiastic adult who imprints his or her
own personality on to the Scheme. Usually also these groups are
in 'closed' communities—schools—where the adults have a control
over the young that is carried across all life. It is not realistic to
suppose that a schoolmaster who is an old-fashioned rigid disciplin-
arian until four o'clock will suddenly turn, at 4.5 pm, into the leader
of a group of volunteers free to go their own way.

A very different sort of Scheme is that done at 17 or 18 for the
Gold. Here the much smaller groups of young people taking part
are acting much more as individuals. If they are still at school they
are in the sixth form, often with responsibility, usually with targets
in the academic world that they must reach in order to progress. If
they are at work they are on the verge of adult life, subject to all the
pressures of money, housing, choice of leisure activities. They are
already being faced with adult choices, and a great many are
thinking from time to time of marriage and their own home. They
have a freedom that the schoolchild cannot imagine. Between these
two categories pressures on the young are such that this bridge is
not easy to cross.

Nor do adults make it easier. The Albemarle Report on the Youth Service noted that not many schools have communications with the youth clubs in their district: teachers do not talk to youth leaders, and so the bridge, if it is crossed, must often be crossed by the young alone.

There are exceptions. One is the Harringay Boys' Club in North London. There the club leader, Mr Tom Ritchie, keeps in touch with the headmaster of a nearby modern school, so boys at that club can do some of their Award activities (such as the fitness tests) organised by the school, and others (such as the expedition) organised by the club. This is how the Scheme is ideally meant to work at the Bronze and Silver levels, providing a bridge for the day when a boy or girl leaves school.

An important factor in the development of the Scheme is going to be the raising of the school-leaving age (which is to go up to 16 in 1970-1, adding an extra 350,000 to the school population in that year). The use of the Award Scheme in schools therefore becomes particularly important. In 1963 the Newsom Report published its findings[1] on the education of children of secondary modern school age and ability.

'Most schools would agree with us', wrote Sir John Newsom and his colleagues, 'in attaching importance to experiences offered outside the formal lesson programme. Already a tremendous range and variety of activities can be found. They include clubs and societies dealing with all kinds of interests: photography, stamp collecting, chess, model-making, boat building, gardening, angling, athletics and sport and games of all kinds; music, including orchestras and choirs, drama and film making—the latter taking very ambitious forms in some schools. There are enthusiastic groups studying local history or a foreign language preparatory to a trip abroad. There are plays and concerts, dances and conferences with neighbouring schools, and a host of enterprises which take place mostly in holiday times or away from school premises—visits, expeditions, camps, holiday journeys and residential courses, including, among most recent developments, educational cruises. The list reflects largely the

1. *Half our Future:* A report of the Central Advisory Council for Education (England). HMSO 1963.

variety of interests and enthusiasms of the teachers who voluntarily direct such activities: it is also an indication of the support
and encouragement given by the local education authority and
by the pupils' parents.'

This, of course, is the picture of an ideal school. If this pattern
were repeated in all schools, if there were enough teachers with a
'variety of interests and enthusiasms', it is fair to say that the
Award Scheme would be superfluous in schools. Alternatively,
teachers welcome the Scheme as a means of creating just this
Newsom atmosphere: for within its framework it encourages all
these activities. But at present there are not enough teachers, with
or without the right qualities. And with the increase in the school
population in 1970 the pressure on schools will become still more
acute.

'Newsom?' one schoolmaster said to me. 'Newsom's fine. But
most of my male colleagues go home at 4.30, have tea and then
start another job—teaching in night schools or running businesses.'

So in the foreseeable future the Award Scheme should be even
more useful in schools, particularly as a means of encouraging
youngsters to do things constructively, which their teachers do not
have time to supervise in detail. But it remains true that the work
of organising the Scheme, and finding additional helpers, must
in schools depend on some teachers. In this situation it is easy to
understand why schoolboys and girls doing the Bronze are often
'persuaded' into pursuits that they are only marginally interested in,
if these can be followed in a group. The shortage of helpers makes
this unavoidable: that, and the natural isolationist views of many
teachers. Overworked, underpaid, and so cut off from the affluence
they see round them, many believe themselves to be the sole
repositories of upright standards and moral values in a decaying
society: so they are even less willing to enlist the help of people
outside the school world in running the Scheme.

Youth clubs have an entirely different problem in running the
Scheme. Their members are volunteers, the clubs have no disciplinary control in the long-term over their members, who can
walk out if they don't like what they find. The Scheme has been
notably successful in a few youth clubs, generally those with strong
leadership and adequate facilities. With the expansion of the Youth

Sir John Hunt, director of the Scheme,
addressing a weekend conference of youth leaders
at Edale, Derbyshire

Gold Award candidates from Surrey
on an expedition across Dartmoor

Photo: Thomas A. Wilkie

The 52-ton yawl *Tawau* which competed in the
1964 Tall Ships Race across the Atlantic.
Half her crew—average age 17—
were holders of the Gold or Silver Awards

Photo: R. T. McNeil

The Award Scheme overseas. Boys from
Machakos School and the Duke of Gloucester School,
Nairobi, resting at the hot springs
in Hell's Gate, Rift Valley, on their Gold Award
expedition

Photo: Willie Alleyne

The first Award winner in Barbados—
Patrol Leader Cecil Grant—receives
his Silver Award from Prince Philip
during his tour in December 1964

'She was an assistant working on the clock
and watch counter when a notice came round
explaining the scheme . . .' Erica Tilbury
of Glasgow

'He really wants to know what we're doing . . .'
Prince Philip with girls at a Birmingham factory

Photo: Birmingham Post and Mail

Prince Philip inspecting a raft made by boys
on a Gold Award training course
at Holt Hall, Norfolk

Photo: Eastern Counties Press, Norwich

Service and the provision of new youth centres in many towns, the prospects for the Scheme are very good indeed. Guildford's planned youth centre, with its areas for engineering and motor-cycle repairing, photography, drama and discussions, is one such imaginative proposal. All these things are possible 'pursuits' in the Award Scheme: and there is no doubt that after one or two expeditions organised from such a centre there will be no shortage of volunteers. But a well-organised youth centre is a very different thing from the back-street youth club, into which boys and girls drift for warmth, comradeship and 'coke'.

Friday night in a public hall on a new housing estate outside a thriving industrial town. The large room is warm, well lit, and in the corner a record player beats out pop tune after pop tune: the Animals, the Stones, the Beatles, heavily recorded to bring up the bass. A hundred or so boys and girls drift up the stairs, pay their sixpences and come in. Some sit in a group of a dozen, in one corner, talking. Others stand round the table-tennis table, and the smallest gyrate like baby storks round the snooker table. A few lean on the 'coke' bar, tapping their feet to the music. Down in the darkened area by the stage, a few pairs shuffle casually round a dance floor: and in one corner two boys and two girls are locked in passionate screen kisses, ignored by everyone else.

In charge—or, rather, keeping an eye on the place—a youth leader in his thirties, much less well dressed than most of the boys and girls with their new sweaters and tight trousers and skirts. 'This place is being closed down after tonight,' said the leader. 'Some of the Education Committee came in last week and they saw a girl on a boy's knee, so they're closing it. I can't see myself that there's much wrong with a girl on a boy's knee, but there you are.' No one at this club would be doing the Award Scheme (though it was here that I met the 16-year-old whose rope broke). But the youth leader's own club, a mile away, did have a range of activities, and any of these youngsters who showed an interest would be invited round there.

'But there are a lot here I wouldn't have in my place,' he said. 'There are two here who've just been inside. It's a great thing to this lot to have been in prison.'

And so, after the closing of that club, the youngsters would go back to the street corners, and breaking up the coffee-bars. These

H

are the ones that the sociologists describe as the 'unattached':
the ones who just don't want to know. What *do* they want? What
do you want when you are young? You want to be accepted by
your friends. You want to contribute to the group, to be noticed.
You want to be independent, in a world that constantly tells you
what to do, at home and at work. And you want to achieve something, to make a mark. If you can't do it any other way you break
a window.

The problem with the majority of young people who will not
relate to the adult world is not that they are bad but that they find
no means to connect. The Crowther Report commented:

'Forty-six per cent of the boys and sixty per cent of the girls
who left modern or all-age schools had no further full-time or
part-time education. But it would be quite wrong to suppose that
education could do nothing more for these boys and girls. To
realise how much undeveloped talent there is in quite ordinary
people one has only to look at the experience of the armed forces.
The job of the present-day infantryman, for instance, calls for an
adaptability and resource which would have surprised the army
of a hundred or even fifty years ago. The challenge produces the
response. Indeed, it was always so. Those occupations, such as
the fisherman's, which have called for more than the average
capability, have found it. The experience of the test expedition
in the Duke of Edinburgh's Award has shown that some boys
whose official intelligence rating is very low have been able
successfully to meet the considerable demands it makes on what
would normally, and rightly, be regarded as intelligence.'[1]

The Scheme can produce better examples than that. There was a
girl in Wales who decided to go in for the Scheme as a member of
a Young Farmers' Club. She was living with her parents in a
derelict cottage. She found that she could take a course in house
purchase, and so she took it. Having studied the subject, she
found that the cost of building or even buying a house for her
parents would be prohibitive, so she discovered a second-hand
pre-fab in good condition, got planning permission to put it on

1. *15 to 18:* Report of the Central Advisory Council for Education (England).
HMSO 1959.

the land next to her parents' cottage, organised and supervised, with her friends, the erection and decoration of the pre-fab, and moved her parents in.

But, say the critics, the trouble is that the Scheme is not presented in terms that appeal to the adolescent. They don't want to climb mountains; they don't want to walk, they want speed. They don't want to cultivate cacti. This, of course misrepresents the Scheme. Some young men have used motor-cycling as a pursuit for the Gold: *Gauntlet* quotes the case of Brian Wright, who was coached by a former West Ham speedway captain 'Tiger' Stevenson. At present in Birmingham new syllabuses are being tried out to cover motor-cycling competitions, scrambles and trials. And soon the Volunteer Emergency Service, a national scheme to provide trained motor-cyclists for such emergencies as the ferrying of blood plasma across country from hospital to hospital, may be added to the service section of the Scheme as a possible qualification.

There is no doubt that young people from many contexts will eagerly help when the need is presented to them. Alec Dickson's Community Service Volunteers, Anthony Stern's groups, work among old people, in mental hospitals and other places where there are staff shortages and which the outside world prefers to forget. This thread of service, incongruously, runs through the stories of young people told in the book *Generation X*. The service section of the Scheme is fully acceptable to young people in its present form, though here again much depends on how it is presented.

The Fire Service and the police are now finding it difficult to provide enough courses to satisfy the demand: in some towns, where the use of the Scheme is increasing, the demand for Award courses in firemanship or police work may become a real problem to services already short-staffed. And here also the leaders have problems. If a course is arranged with the police, and the course turns out to be a jolly and undemanding series of fireside chats on the lines of *Z Cars*, who is to tell the organisers that this isn't what the Scheme was intended to be? When people are putting themselves out to help it is often difficult to reject such help on the grounds that it isn't what was wanted. Ideally, such courses would be prepared in depth, and discussed beforehand with all the operating authorities: this is not always practicable and so at the

Bronze and Silver stages the element of challenge is sometimes lacking in the Service course.

To some extent provision of this sort must remain haphazard, because life is like that. Who is to measure whether a young steel-worker, going once a week to help in a club for spastics, is learning more about service to others than a schoolboy who sits in a police station looking at slides of burglaries?

What elements in the Scheme, then, can be changed to bring them up to date and make them appealing to adolescents? Some will no doubt jib at the expedition. At present the Gold expedition can be done (by boys) 'on foot . . . by cycle, canoe, sailing or on skis or horseback'. Possibly one day a Gold expedition might be done on a motor-bike or scooter, provided only that the expedition was adequately prepared for, and that the candidate slept out under canvas or in the open for the necessary three nights. But the motor-bike intrudes on other people's lives, where it is often unwelcome, in a way that the walker or cyclist does not.

There comes a point when a Scheme such as this can no longer be adjusted without changing its character altogether. There is probably a number of young men who would regard sleeping out in this way as not 'switched on'. But there must be many others who, having done it because the Scheme required it, found they enjoyed it. To a certain extent the Scheme must always offer experiences that are beyond the imagination of those attempting it: much of the point of it is that young people are thus enabled to tackle challenges they never believed they could answer. If the expedition were merely an adult imposition there would be an argument for changing its character: but the enthusiasm for it I have found among all sorts of boys and girls who have done it convinces me that it is right.

But here once more there is an uneven amount of effort. I was told of caches of camping equipment in police cadet headquarters, where the latest lavish anoraks, boots and rucksacks are issued out free to cadets for their expeditions—while elsewhere boys are saving up their money to buy the minimum equipment for themselves. Until youth centres are more richly financed there is no solution to this: one can only say that the police cadets have a head start.

How else can the Scheme be made to appeal? It is true that apart from the 'pursuits' and 'service' sections, the Boys' Scheme is often seen as principally a physical challenge, and a boy can win a Gold Award on two-thirds sport and expedition. But the expedition demands careful planning and forethought, and for the service a Gold candidate must perform a period of public service. This in itself is doubtless a good thing socially, but it does little to 'broaden interests'. It is a possible criticism of the Scheme, as administered in some places, that what the Albemarle Report said of youth clubs could also be said of the Boys' Awards: that 'it is easy for youth clubs and organisations to acquire a general philistinism without knowing it'.

Yet this is not a failure of the Scheme: it is a failure of the operating authorities. Personally I do not consider that a grammar school boy who is using some form of sport as his 'pursuit' for the Gold is fulfilling the spirit of the Scheme, even though he may be well within the letter: though I appreciate the argument that boys in an academic world need all the encouragement to recreation that they can get.

The Scheme's difficulties are not with grammar school boys, but with those who leave school at 15. How can it appeal to them? First of all, anything that is provided must not play down to some imaginary lowered standard. There is ample proof that young people respond to enthusiasm in all fields. Michael Croft has built his National Youth Theatre not from brilliant young natural actors but from ordinary boys and girls. Each year the *Sunday Mirror* exhibition of children's art and the *Daily Mirror* book of writing by young authors prove that the schools have many teachers who elicit a creative response. The boys and girls of South Wales, presented with the details of the Scheme during citizenship courses at Coleg-y-Fro, the YMCA college, have eagerly responded to it.

Almost anything can be made to appeal if it is presented attractively by an enthusiastic adult. In South Wales there has been a noteworthy outbreak of archaeology and local history among the young, sparked off by Cardiff Museum's plan to map and survey the valleys. There have been many instances of individual boys and girls who have found great fun and interest in local history and topography, a field in which there are many adult helpers. Though not all candidates reach the standard of Anthony Jones, whose scholarly and wittily illustrated survey of chapel architecture in his native Merthyr Tydfil was very properly published by the local council.

But the body of 15- to 18-year-olds have their own interests, often intense but as often momentary, the 'crazes' of the young. For this age group the Girls' Awards are more immediately attractive in many ways than the Boys', with much broader interests. The Design for Living section, with its courses in make-up and hair styles and home-making, can be seen to be attractive by every girl. It should be possible to devise something on these lines for the Boys' Awards, though the difficulties are obvious.

First, because not every boy of 17, even if he thinks of marriage, thinks seriously about such practical details as finding or buying a home, arranging a mortgage, and so on. The girls do. And, secondly, because the other great interest of many boys, clothes, do not have an easily administered link with the adult world. Many boys, even the 'unattached', know the correct shape and height for a young man's shoe if he is 'switched on'; many would have strong views on the correctness or uncorrectness of a pop star's high-collared and polka-dot shirts. But who in the adult world is competent to run a course in clothes for young men? Only perhaps the tycoons of Carnaby Street.

But a good and useful course could be worked out for boys, dealing with the wearing qualities of different cloths and how to judge these qualities, the washability and wearing qualities of man-made fibres, and how to wash, drip-dry and fold a shirt. But would there be enough schoolmasters or youth leaders to take such a course seriously?

However, most of these young men in the early years of their married life will have wives who are at work: more than a few would find it an advantage to be able to cook (and so would their wives). The boys should be able to take a course, as the girls can, in electricity in the home.

The girls over 17 may take a course on The Girl, the Boy, and Marriage. There is no equivalent in the Boys' Award. If there was one, would enough qualified people be found to run it? And how, when the standards of sexual morality are no longer commonly agreed, even in the adult world, could any course be planned that would mean the same thing to all young people?

It might be possible to popularise the Scheme still further by adopting the rosy nirvana of the advertising world and running a campaign to show that Award winners get the prettiest girls ('Go bold—go Gold!'). But there are two factors that will either carry the Scheme forward or frustrate it. The first is the interest of the adults who must in the first place present the Scheme to young people as an opportunity worth taking. If it is put forward in the guise of yet another obstacle course contrived by adults to test the young and make them conform to established social patterns it will draw an annual quota of polite young participants and become familiar, and dead.

The second factor is the leadership of those who have taken part in the Scheme. Few can lead the young so well as the young themselves. It is when the Gold Award winner gets his picture in the paper and wears Prince Philip's badge that his juniors start to look and listen and wonder whether they could earn it too. In every group there is a leader. Gangs and clubs both function through committees and discussions, but they take fire and start to do things when one or two leading characters grasp the initiative.

The young are often criticised because their excitement is superficial and their thrills purposeless. The same could be said of a great many adult pleasures. But there are many young people, probably the majority, who are looking for something to do that they can call 'real'. It is no good telling them that they will find it in serving the elderly or the handicapped. But if they see one of their personal heroes doing it they will want to join in: and, having joined in, they will work eagerly and selflessly.

The Duke of Edinburgh has earned the respect and affection of the young not so much by anything he has said (though they admire his plain speaking) but what they can see he has done. They use the youth clubs and playing fields that have been provided, as they recognise, through his hard and relentless pressure. Even those young men and women who would claim to have no time for rank and status are proud to wear his badge. His leadership is something real because he has not ordered them to do anything: he has challenged them to do something, and they have accepted the challenge, and won.

In their turn the Award winners often take up a further challenge. They take on responsibility, in their own towns, for youth work and social service in many forms. They become leaders among their own generation by virtue of what they have done. They become, through experience, the sort of men and women that other youngsters respect and look to for advice: because the quality of 'stickability' is something that mankind responds to when it is exercised for the general good.

The Scheme has grown in ten years from an experimental pilot venture among young people into a nation-wide (and almost world-wide) challenge. In these ten years it has proved beyond any doubt that the young people of Britain are vigorous, lively, imaginative and creative. On the hills, in the schools, the youth clubs, the factories, offices, shops and banks the Duke of Edinburgh's challenge has been taken up. The challenge produces the response.

Appendices

Appendix 1

Outline of conditions—the Boys' Awards

	SERVICE	EXPEDITIONS
BRONZE for those between 14 and 17	Train in one form of service, eg First Aid, Lifesaving, Help in Emergencies, etc.	Fifteen-mile expedition *on foot only* (one night camping out)
SILVER for those between 15 and 18	Further training to a higher standard	Thirty-mile expedition on foot (two nights camping out) or a comparable journey by cycle, canoe, sailing, or on skis or horseback
GOLD for those between 16 and 20	Further training to a higher standard	Fifty-mile expedition on foot (three nights camping out) *in wild country*, or a comparable journey by cycle, canoe, sailing, or on skis or horseback

NOTE: It is possible to enter the Scheme at each stage, on certain conditions. A more detailed account of these conditions, and of the variations in the Scheme generally, may be found in the *Boys' Leaders' Handbook* (1965 edition), available from the Award Offices, price 1s. 6d.

PURSUITS AND INTERESTS	PHYSICAL FITNESS	ADDITIONAL REQUIREMENTS FOR *GOLD* *AWARDS*
Follow one pursuit for a period of six months	Pass in three out of five groups, to Bronze standards, eg 100 yds—13 secs	
Follow one pursuit for a further period of six months	As for Bronze, but to higher standards, eg 100 yds—12·2 secs	
Follow one pursuit for a further period of twelve months	Pass in three out of six groups to Gold standards, eg 100 yds—11·8 secs	Practical service to the community Residential qualification

Outline of conditions—the Girls' Awards

	DESIGN FOR LIVING	PURSUITS AND INTERESTS
BRONZE for those between 14 and 20	One activity from —Grooming and Poise —Setting up your home —Running your house Syllabus on 'Good manners'	One interest pursued for six months
SILVER for those between 15 and 20 *Work done for the Bronze counts towards the Silver*	Two activities from —Grooming and Poise —Setting up your home —Running your home or one activity at a higher level Syllabus on 'Good manners'	Two interests for six months each, or one interest for twelve months
GOLD for those between 16 and 20 *Work done for the Silver counts towards the Gold*	Three activities from —Grooming and Poise —Setting up your home —Running your home taken at different levels Syllabus on 'Good manners'	Three interests over varying periods, or two interests for twelve months each

NOTE: It is possible to enter the Scheme at each stage, on certain conditions. A more detailed account of these conditions, and of the variations in the Scheme generally, may be found in the *Girls' Leaders' Handbook* (1965 edition), available from the Award Offices, price 1s. 6d.

ADVENTURE	SERVICE	ADDITIONAL REQUIREMENTS FOR *GOLD* *AWARD*
Basic training and a day's journey	Training in one service from Mothercraft and Child Care, Life Saving, Care of Animals, Voluntary Service and Help in Emergencies	
Basic training, a day's journey and an expedition of one night and two days	Training in two forms of service, or one at a higher level	
Basic training, a day's journey, an expedition of one night and two days, and an expedition of five nights and six days *or* voluntary help with some special worthwhile project	Training in two forms of service, at a higher level	Syllabus of training in everyday nursing Six months' voluntary service to the community Attendance at a residential course of at least four nights and five days

Subjects for Pursuits and Interests

Each of these subjects may represent one quarter of an Award, at Bronze, Silver or Gold standard. So no boy or girl gets an Award solely for cacti cultivation: but if he or she reaches the required standard in physical fitness or Design for Living, an expedition, and a form of service, he or she may qualify for an Award by taking a measurable interest in any one of these subjects for six months (for Bronze or Silver) or twelve months for boys and six months for girls (for the Gold). The syllabuses are intended solely as guidance, and do not necessarily indicate any definite standard of achievement. Each syllabus suggests a programme to be followed by candidates possessing varying degrees of experience, proficiency and maturity, listed under the headings:

For beginners
For those with some knowledge
For the more advanced

Opposite are some examples from the list. Sample draft syllabuses are reproduced on pages 132 and 133:

Many of the subjects for pursuits and interests may be taken by both boys and girls, but, in addition, the girls include other activities some of which are:

Aero Modelling
Agriculture
Archery
Architectural Appreciation
Art Appreciation
Astronomy
Ballet Appreciation
Bee-keeping
Bible Study
Boatwork
Braille
Cacti cultivation
Canoeing
Cars—Model and Electric
Caving and Pot-holing
Chess
Chinchillas
Civics
Cookery at Home
Dancing:
Ballet
Ballroom
English Folk
Modern Educational
Old Time
National
Scottish Country or Highland
Welsh Folk
Driving—Motor-car,
motor-cycle or scooter

Fancy Ropework
Fishing
Gardening
Golf
Heraldry
Hygiene (including Food
Handling)
Jazz
Judo
Languages
Local and Historical survey
Magazine Production
Marksmanship
Music:
Buglers and Trumpeters
Drummers
Guitar playing
Piping
Wind Instrument
Ornithology
Period Furniture
Photography
Riding
Rowing
Screen Printing
Skating—Ice and Roller
Umpiring/Refereeing
Wine Making
Woodcarving
Zoology

Athletics
Basketry
Crocheting
Dressmaking
Educational gymnastics
Embroidery

Fabric Printing
Knitting
Patchwork
Pillow Lace Making
Soft-toy Making
Skipping

Appendix 4

Two Specimen Draft Syllabuses

The Scheme demands that young people shall 'take an interest' in some subject for a certain period of time. So that adult helpers may have a yardstick to measure 'interest', which is in many activities almost incapable of being accurately measured by standards that would be generally applicable, the Scheme has produced draft syllabuses for several dozen 'interests'.

The two given here have been chosen arbitrarily to illustrate the lines of approach recommended by the Scheme in two very different subjects—Civics, and Driving (Motor-cycle or Scooter).

1. Civics   This syllabus is for guidance only. The principle of assessment in this section is the interest, progress and genuine sustained effort shown by the candidate during the stipulated period, not the attainment of any fixed standard.
N.B. Girls may not attempt more than TWO levels.

For beginners   The candidate should be familiar with the general meaning of the term 'Society' and of the conditions upon which men have learned to live together in harmony.
   The candidate should have a working knowledge of the organisation of his/her local community, and should:
   1. Draw a map of the area showing the location of all main services: hospital, fire station, police station, local government offices, schools, public library, at least one doctor, the district nurse, etc.
   2. Draw a chart showing the structure of his/her Local Authority (Borough, Urban District, Rural District, County Council, etc.)
   3. Have a general knowledge of the function of the officers of this Authority, and a more detailed knowledge of the work of any one senior official preferably making personal contact.
   4. Study and be able to give an account of official and voluntary services to the community in the neighbourhood.
   5. Show evidence of active help given to one of the local social agencies.

For those with
some
knowledge   He or she should possess an elementary appreciation of those forces which operate to sustain society and those which tend to destroy it.
   Candidates should:
   1. Show a working knowledge of the administration of his/her locality, together with an understanding of how this is financed.
   2. Attend several local council meetings, and give a written account of the business transacted.
   3. Have a general knowledge of his/her Parliamentary Constituency and its representation.
   4. Know how local problems can be raised in public, e.g. through the local council, the local newspaper, M.P., etc.

5. Have knowledge of the local court(s) and its/their working.

6. Know the privileges and duties of the Lord Lieutenant, and Sheriff.

7. Show further evidence of active help and if possible of administrative or Committee work with one of the local agencies.

For the more advanced

Candidate should:

1. *National:*

Have a general knowledge of the composition and working of Parliament and the Franchise.

Understand the powers of government organs of constitution and their functions, processes of legislation and taxation, the relationship between the Executive and the Administration, the Government and the State, and have a knowledge of the concept and administration of justice in this country.

2. *International:*

Study the development of an international body of nations, e.g. UNO, NATO, EFTA, The British Commonwealth of Nations. Be able to explain in general terms the reason for such supernational organisations.

The candidate should give evidence of having read consistently a daily newspaper, presenting a scrap book of cuttings on some national or international matter, and should work out a practical project under guidance of the tutor.

2. Driving— Motor-cycle or scooter

This syllabus is for guidance only. The principle of assessment in this Section is the interest, progress and genuine sustained effort shown by the candidate during the stipulated period, not the attainment of any fixed standard.

N.B. Girls may not attempt more than TWO levels. This syllabus, however, includes certain requirements for the candidate's safety and these must be followed.

Age: In law a person under 16 years of age cannot be in possession of a driving licence of any kind.

For beginners

1. The candidate must be the holder of a valid provisional driving licence.

2. The candidate will be expected to be reasonably proficient in the following:

(*a*) Knowledge of the Highway Code, with emphasis on hand signals and Ministry of Transport road signs.

(*b*) Knowledge of the law relating to motor-cycles or scooters in regard to driving licences, certificates of insurance, excise licences and construction and use of regulations.

(*c*) Knowledge of the principles of braking and acceleration.

(*d*) Knowledge of the principles of two- and four-stroke engines.

(*e*) Knowledge of the main causes of accidents involving motor-cyclists and scooterists.

3. The candidate will be expected to drive a motor-cycle or scooter round a two-mile test circuit which will include some heavy traffic, uncontrolled cross roads, mandatory traffic signs, right-hand turns, a pedestrian crossing.

The candidate will be examined on:

(*a*) Observation—particularly to the rear.
(*b*) Hand signals.
(*c*) Positioning.
(*d*) Gear changing.
(*e*) Machine control.
(*f*) Consideration for other road users.
(*g*) Prompt and correct action on all signals.
(*h*) Emergency stop.
(*i*) Overtaking.

4. The candidate must prove his/her skill in balance, braking throttle control, and the intelligent use of the clutch at low and speeds by taking the following tests:

(*a*) Gradient tests: in a 1:6 gradient, stop engine and re-start without any assistance other than the use of brakes. (The machine must not be allowed to slip backwards.)
(*b*) Figures of Eight test: a series of figures of eight should be performed with feet on footrests in a clearly defined 18 ft wide lane with two obstacles 12 ft apart.
(*c*) Obstacles test: six obstacles placed 9 ft apart in a straight line or 11 ft apart for scooters and the candidate asked to negotiate these.

5. The candidate should pass the Ministry of Transport Group 'G' driving test.

For those with some knowledge

1. The candidate must have held a valid Group 'G' driving licence for at least six months.
2. If the candidate has not taken the first level he or she must be tested on those points in that level, not in the following tests.
3. The candidate will be expected to be reasonably proficient in the following:
(*a*) Knowledge of the construction and adjustment of two- and four-stroke carburettors.
(*b*) Knowledge of lubricating system, oil checking routine and oil changes.
(*c*) Repairs such as removing wheel and mending punctures, cleaning and adjusting the points of a sparking plug, clearing petrol chokes, adjustment of brakes.
(*d*) Planning routes with the aid of maps and guide books.
4. The candidates will be expected to carry out a scheduled journey of 100 miles of which fifty miles will be during daylight on 'B' class and unclassified roads and fifty miles during darkness on 'A' class roads.

For the more advanced

1. The candidate must have held a valid group 'G' driving licence for a further period of twelve months.
2. The candidate will be expected to be reasonably proficient in the following:
(*a*) Knowledge of electrical systems on motor-cycles or scooters and be able to trace electrical faults.
(*b*) Knowledge of the working of clutch and gear box.
3. The candidate will be expected to carry out a scheduled journey of 200 miles: 100 miles in daylight on 'B' and unclassified roads, including a steep hill climb and descent during which time a new tyre and tube will be fitted; and 100 miles during darkness on 'A' class roads during which time a fault in the electrical wiring system will be rectified.

NOTES

1. At all three stages the candidate should wear suitable clothing, including gloves, goggles, and must wear a safety helmet.
2. Suggested test books:
Roadcraft, published by Her Majesty's Stationery Office.
Good Riding, published by The Royal Society for the Prevention of Accidents.
Know the Game Series—Motor Cycling.

New entrants to the Scheme

	Boys	Girls
1957	7,000	—
1958	10,000	—
1959	13,000	3,700
1960	26,000	4,500
1961	35,000	7,300
1962	42,000	18,500
1963	43,300	19,600
1964	41,360	18,400

Awards granted

		Gold	Silver	Bronze	Total
1957	Boys	—	315	756	1,071
1958	Boys	82	784	1,718	2,584
1959	Boys	217	1,386	2,453	4,056
	Girls	15	100	750	865
1960	Boys	361	2,143	4,093	6,597
	Girls	57	240	1,130	1,427
1961	Boys	920	3,891	6,716	11,527
	Girls	133	530	1,962	2,625
1962	Boys	1,333	4,920	9,248	15,501
	Girls	169	832	3,819	4,820
1963	Boys	1,673	6,000	9,784	17,457
	Girls	330	1,281	5,221	6,832
1964	Boys	2,087	6,425	9,671	18,183
	Girls	422	1,615	6,546	8,583
		7,799	30,462	63,867	102,128

List of Benefactors

As well as a number of anonymous donors,
the Trustees are grateful to:

Charles Abrahams Esq.
Gerald Abrahams Esq.
Alcan Industries Ltd
Allied Breweries Ltd
All Saints College, New South Wales
Hardy Amies Esq.
Anglo-Amalgamated Film Distributors Ltd & their associates overseas
Aquascutum Ltd
Armourers' & Braziers' Company
Arsenal Football Club Ltd
Associated Television Ltd
Avon India Rubber Co.
Lady Balcon
Bank of London & South America Ltd
Barr Muir & Co. Ltd
British Broadcasting Corporation (TV Centre)
Bekhor, Renton & Co.
S. H. Benson Ltd
Blackpool North Shore Golf Club
Blin & Blin Ltd
Neville Blond Esq.
Bovril Ltd
Bridge in Britain
British Insulated Callender's Cables Ltd
British Leather Federation
British Motor Corporation Group Facilities Ltd
British Nylon Spinners Ltd
British Petroleum Co. Ltd
British Trades Alphabet Ltd
Sir William Butlin, MBE
Cadbury Brothers Ltd
W. A. Cadbury Trust
J. Cawthra & Co. Ltd
Charrington & Co. Ltd
City Parochial Foundation

Cochran & Clark
Alfred S. Cohen Charitable Trust
B. Cohen (Morada) Ltd
Nat Cohen Esq.
Mrs R. Cole
L. P. Conduit Esq.
Co-operative Insurance Society Ltd
Courage Barclay & Simonds Ltd
Augustine Courtauld
—Do Good Fund
E. E. Crabtree Esq.
Cresta Silks Ltd
Crompton Parkinson Ltd
J. B. Crowther & Sons (Milnsbridge) Ltd
The Daily Sketch
Dannimac (Manufacturing) Ltd
Dartington Hall Ltd
Debenhams Charity Trust
Department of Education & Science
Dulverton Trust
Dulwich College Preparatory School
Dunlop Rubber Co. Ltd
Esso Petroleum Co. Ltd
The Evening News
Express Dairy Co. Ltd
G. J. Fairhead Esq.
Mrs Featherstone
Fenwick Ltd
Fisher & Ludlow Ltd
Floris Bakeries Ltd
Football Association
Forte's (Holdings) Ltd
J. S. Fry & Sons Ltd
R. Gaskell Esq.
Gilbeys Ltd
Gillette Industries Ltd
John Gladstone & Co. Ltd
The Goldsmiths' Company
Mrs F. Goldstein

Index